YOUTH PLANNING CHARRETTES

A Manual for Planners, Teachers, and Youth Advocates

Bruce Race, AICP, AIA

and

Carolyn Torma

Planners Press
American Planning Association
Chicago, Illinois   Washington, D.C.

Copyright 1998 by the American Planning Association
122 S. Michigan Ave., Suite 1600, Chicago, IL 60603

ISBN 1-884829-19-8
Library of Congress Catalog Card Number 98-73601

Printed in the United States of America

TABLE OF CONTENTS

This book was written as a resource for planners and educators working with young citizens. It provides advice on how to design a process that is informed and interactive, where youth own the results and are empowered to act as advocates for their issues. The book focuses on the role of workshops and charrettes in the planning and educational process. The charrette is one of the most powerful tools for allowing young people to come to a collective understanding of their issues, and the options and actions available to them.

As the authors, we believe that no charrette is truly successful without the blending of educational objectives and real-life, problem-solving objectives. Therefore, we recommend that teachers and planners work together on these projects whether they take place in the school or in another setting. The strengths, skills, and insights that each group of professionals brings to the charrette is needed. Professional teachers understand their students, how they learn, the context of their experience, and the appropriate techniques and level of understanding needed in an educational event. Professional planners understand the content of planning and its related social issues. They understand how cities function and they possess the skills for group facilitation and collaborative problem solving. Youth participants will feel most receptive to new experiences when they have the excitement of working on something new and the comfort of knowing the new experience will be placed within the context of their overall education.

INTRODUCTION
The Power and Insights of Young People
Several principles that have developed from the authors' experiences as planners and educators guide this book. The manner in which we approach charrettes is based on these principles.

- Young people are capable of discerning problems, making decisions, and actively participating in the solutions for the development of their communities.
- Planning processes that involve youth must be sincere in both incorporating youth and in implementing their suggestions; the process should not be used simply for public relations.
- The charrette should be as fully participatory and democratic as possible.
- The charrette and planning process should convey an understanding of the civic process and avoid portraying an idealist's world in which every problem is solved instantly to each person's satisfaction. In short, we believe that young people can accept a truthful education experience.

Youth can bring clear and intelligent insights into the planning process. Whether it is how a community's open space system should be planned or the revitalization of a shopping district, young people offer amazing energy and perspective on contemporary planning issues in America. By becoming active citizens, youth can become empowered, informed, and active participants in the community planning process. A workshop and charrette process is an effective method used by

In San Diego, students from Zamorano Elementary School tackled the problem of making a transitional warehouse and commercial district into a neighborhood more friendly for children and their families.

educators and community planners to include youth as active citizens.

THE BENEFITS OF INVOLVING YOUTH IN PLANNING

The process of planning provides hands-on experience for young people that supports a number of educational and empowerment objectives. Whether this involves citizenship awareness, real advocacy, social or civic studies, young people gain from this involvement, both learning and expressing a vision of their future.

Charrettes can sharpen communication and analytical skills by using well-established classroom education techniques such as drawing, writing, photography, survey design, group problem-solving, and public speaking. Perhaps most appealing, charrettes offer the opportunity for students to apply to the world, in an innovative way, what they learn in school.

Active Citizenship

Many community-based organizations immerse young people in planning efforts that are geared to provide real life advocacy regarding urban issues. The youth participants learn to identify their issues, conduct research, explore alternatives, and advocate solutions. They can even become involved in the implementation of the selected solutions to community problems. They become active citizens using the "learn-by-doing" method.

Youth Empowerment

Young people can be empowered by the planning experience. They gain a voice in community affairs by being able to articulate a position, back it up with information, and express a course of action. They become credible and influential citizens.

Urban, Social, and Civic Studies

In a school setting, the introduction of planning lessons or projects can provide insights into the anatomy and working of government and cities. This can increase young peoples' understanding of how urban issues and problems are interrelated. Further, young participants learn the vocabulary of public decision making. In addition, a rich variety of skills and subjects can be used in planning education, including writing, math, drawing, and public speaking.

The Learning Process

Perhaps the greatest benefit for young people is the experience of analyzing information, organizing ideas, and communicating findings. As the planning process or project moves through stages of discovery, identifying problems, analyzing solutions, deciding on a course of action, and implementation, young planners/participants experience the process of public decision making. They learn how to define the problem, establish goals, explore alternatives, and advocate solutions. The workshop and charrette are powerful tools in this learning process.

Community Education Services (CES) is a program of San Francisco's Chinatown Wellness Village Planning Program. It provided youth an opportunity to design and manage a planning process.

DEFINING THE PROCESS:
YOUTH WORKSHOPS AND CHARRETTES

In this book, the term *charrette* (French for cart) is defined as a process in which youth participate in activities that define issues, and find solutions to community planning and urban design problems. Most charrettes take place within a concentrated period of time with participants working non-stop on solving the problem. Several things distinguish the charrette from other techniques of instruction.

◆ The charrette addresses a real problem rather than a hypothetical one.
◆ The research done on the problem uses actual, not hypothetical, information.

Citizen participation in issues sometimes means protests. In this case, citizens of all ages joined in a demonstration against toxic emissions in a community in Ohio. Public speech is one important way of advocating a position. Planning seeks to involve citizens in decision making so that confrontations like these are not necessary.

Commonly Used Terms in this Book

Issues. These are a related set of problems that appear to develop from a common set of causes. For example, "poor air quality" is an issue that springs from the problems of: not enough efficient and appealing mass transit; too many incentives for using one's personal car, such as cheap and plentiful parking, and inexpensive gas; high density populations; and environmental conditions that trap smog.

Policy. Policy is a set of official actions, or non-actions, that affect issues. For example, a policy that encourages the expansion of superhighways in and around a community may increase poor air quality. A policy that encourages bicycling and mass transit may improve air quality.

Advocacy. This is the action that someone will take to influence a policy and the decisions that support that policy. For example, a clean air advocate may conduct a public information rally to increase the public's awareness of the causes of poor air quality and its health consequences.

Community-based organization. Many communities have organizations that address particular community problems. These CBOs may receive funding from government, foundations, or individuals and operate independently of government agencies. An example of this is Shelter Partnerships, Inc., which advocates and helps to develop assistance programs for the homeless.

Public participation. City and regional planning practice mandates that the public be involved in the planning process. Traditionally, this has meant that the public was invited to attend a public meeting to discuss issues. However, planners have developed many creative approaches to participation, from the high-tech approach of an Electronic Town Meeting to the broad goal-setting approach called visioning.

Visioning. A recent form of community goal setting, visioning attempts to involve the entire community in a public discussion about what the community values about itself and how it wishes to evolve into the future. Visioning has sometimes been used as a quicker and less cumbersome approach to the comprehensive plan.

Sponsor or Client. A client is the person for whom the planning recommendations are being made or addressed. For example, the city council could be the client for the plan young people develop in a charrette. In this work, the word *sponsor* is used interchangeably with *client* to mean much the same thing. A slightly more precise definition of sponsor is a group that actively supports the charrette, and is interested in the results (such as a museum), but may not be the audience to whom the plan is addressed.

Facilitator. This is the person leading the charrette and managing the live event. This person often is also the charrette leader and organizer.

Kids' Assistant. This is any adult participating in the charrette and working with the young people. It could be a volunteer planner, teacher, or museum educator. The reason for the name is to emphasize the primacy of the kids as the idea generators.

Prompter Question. Used by the facilitator or the kids' assistants to help stimulate young people to think more deeply about an observation, idea, or recommendation, prompter questions are used throughout the charrette to stimulate thought.

- The process is structured so that all members of the group participate in the process.
- Adults help facilitate, but do not provide answers or a fixed view of what should happen.
- The youth participants are asked to develop solutions to the problem.

Charrettes involve many skills and learning techniques, including:

- Research and analysis of information
- Drawing and mapping
- Observation and recording
- Photography and graphic design
- Group problem solving
- Project or exhibit development
- Oral presentation

Originating in the field of architecture, charrettes serve as creative brainstorming sessions. Often celebrity professionals are brought into the community for the charrette and help bring publicity to an issue. But you don't need imported talent to generate excitement and attention—the novelty of children's participation in community problem solving will often draw media attention. Youth planning charrettes can also engage parents in the planning process through the excitement generated by their children's work.

For many of us, charrettes may be most familiar as exercises to bring awareness to an issue. As a publicity tactic, the charrette is often not part of an official or adopted planning process. However, many planners are beginning to see the value of incorporating them as a creative and engaging form of public participation. In this book, we recommend using them for both teaching and as integral parts of the planning process. Quite obviously, most planning problems cannot be solved in a one-day charrette event; the charrette must be part of a larger set of programs that address the planning issues.

SHORT OVERVIEW OF THE FIELD OF PLANNING

For those readers who are not planners, a little background on city planning is helpful. Although most planners call their field *planning*, many try to define the field more precisely by calling it *city and regional planning*. Still other planners are most comfortable with the term *community planning*. Here is a brief overview of the history, profession, and process of planning.

The Practice of Planning

"The application of forethought to action" is how Stuart Meck, AICP, former president of the

One of the most famous town plans in America is of Washington, D.C. Designed by Pierre Charles L'Enfant in 1790, the plan incorporated long, open malls that provide axial vistas of major monuments and radiating streets. These features were adapted by L'Enfant from European Baroque town planning.

History

Planning as a field is almost 90 years old. As planning historian John Reps notes, the "field of city planning grew out of the land-based professions of architecture, engineering, surveying, and landscape architecture, as well as from the work of economists, social workers, lawyers, public health specialists, and municipal administrators." Organized as a profession in 1917, the first association was called the American City Planning Institute. Frederick L. Olmsted, Jr. was the first *(Continued on page xi)*

American Planning Association, defines planning. The goal of city and regional planning is to further the welfare of people and their communities by creating communities that "work." Planners usually use the term *community* to define what it is they are planning. In reality, planners plan for cities, neighborhoods or districts within cities, as well as villages, counties, states, regions, federal agencies, and rural areas. In this book, we use the term *community* to encompass all these types of planning.

Planners seek to develop a well-planned community that:

◆ Provides equal access for its members to homes and jobs.
◆ Provides for the needs of its neediest members.
◆ Is designed and managed to promote the health of its residents.
◆ Is designed to provide services that are efficient, safe, and attractive.
◆ Serves the needs of both the present and future generations.

Planners produce a product, called the *plan*, but are equally concerned with how the plan is created. In this book, we refer to this as *the planning process*. Therefore, planners are responsible for both the plan and an effective planning process. The formal plan is a public document that summarizes:

◆ Analysis of the community.
◆ Analysis of specific topics, such as housing.
◆ Established and agreed-upon goals.
◆ Established and agreed-upon rules for community development.
◆ Established tools to guide its development. Some examples of this include: zoning, special tax programs, and historic preservation incentives.
◆ Proposed alternative strategies to future development.
◆ Recommended methods for implementing the plan.

The Planning Process

Planning follows a series of distinct steps, and this is reflected in the elements of the plan. The charrette process, therefore, will also follow this general outline.

◆ The vision and establishing goals
◆ Assessing the community and its resources (research)
◆ Identifying the problems
◆ Examining the possible solutions to problems
◆ Creating tools for addressing the problems
◆ Establishing a course of action through a plan
◆ Implementing the plan

As this drawing by Sarout Long in San Francisco illustrates, learning about the steps in the planning process helps empower young people. They learn how public policy is established and how their efforts can be thoughtful and credible contributions to that policy.

While the ideal planning process focuses on the creation of a plan, most planners work on short-term projects or in the administration of established programs. In these instances, they operate from a more informal agreement than the comprehensive plan, such as a project proposal. Many consulting planners work on new suburban subdivision developments. Others administer specific land-use programs, such as zoning or historic building designation. Still others provide information and technical assistance for programs such as neighborhood planning, housing, or transportation. A good comprehensive plan will provide the framework for this work and should guide public decisions. The role of the planner in each of these working situations is to provide:

◆ A broad perspective on community issues.
◆ Updates to both community members and officials on the process.

(Continued from page x)
president–his father was the world-famous landscape architect, F.L. Olmsted.

Cities have existed for thousands of years. The design of cities was created by many types of individuals. Religious leaders created cathedral towns, bishoprics, and holy cities, such as Mecca. Military leaders created Roman cities all across Western Europe, and other military leaders created forts and fortresses around the world, from Ukraine to Canada. In the United States, engineers designed railroad towns across the American continent. Many common town designs, such as county seat towns, were developed and platted by land surveyors. Kings, queens, emperors and their officials gave form to cities such as Versailles, France, and the Forbidden City in Beijing, China.

In smaller communities there is usually no record of a specific town designer. Some communities grew from clusters of farms or fishermen's buildings or commercial businesses erected on the edges of religious compounds. Land use and land ownership patterns, cultivation patterns, cultural and religious customs, and the economic livelihood of the residents gave rise to distinctive forms of small communities in all parts of the world.

The modern profession of planning addresses the full range of city planning issues from social issues, such as public housing, to urban design issues, such as greenways along the community river. Much of contemporary city planning focuses on land use and regulation. Visit APA's web site at *www.planning.org* for a short overview of American planning history. Entitled *Pathways in American Planning History*, the specific address is *www.planning.org/info/intro.*

Types of Plans

Planners develop many different kinds of plans. When describing what they do, most planners describe the comprehensive plan. However, the range of plans they produce runs from comprehensive, communitywide plans to historic district preservation plans. More specialized plans are often more simple and are produced more quickly than a comprehensive plan. These may include a plan for the downtown Main Street, neighborhood, or regional transportation. Here are some fictional examples:

- Strategic Plan for Downtown Houston Economic Development
- Redevelopment Plan for the Wacker Tot Lot
- Comprehensive Plan for the City of Denver
- Vision 20/20: Seattle in the Year 2020
- Cedar Hills Historic District Preservation Plan
- Park Recreation Plan for the Village of Falls River
- I-60 Corridor Plan for Biggerton County
- A Plan for Tornado Disaster Response in Lincoln
- State Historic Preservation Plan for South Dakota
- Blackstone River and Canal Heritage and Redevelopment Plan

- Technical information.
- Facilitation of the legal and democratic process in which decisions are made.

Creating the Vision and Establishing Goals. Planners work within a highly collaborative process. Through this collaborative process, in which many different groups of people participate, planners define the community's goals for itself. Planners refer to this process as *visioning*. The vision expresses what community members:

- Wish their community to look like today and in the future.
- Want in terms of services and protections.
- Want to do to address problems.
- Want to emphasize as goals for its political leaders to strive toward.

Planners work with local residents, politicians, business people, government professionals, and special groups, such as neighborhood or environmental groups, in developing a vision for the community. Within the profession there is an ongoing debate about whether planners should be advocates for particular ideas and issues or should be neutral. In the latter view, planners should simply facilitate or manage a process in which others decide the issues and the solutions to problems. It is more likely that a planner who works in a nonprofit or community-based organization will serve as an advocate, and the planner in government will define his or her role as the manager of the process.

Where Planning Is Done and Who Does Planning. In this book, planning is explored primarily at the local community level. As mentioned before, however, planners work with many types of communities, from neighborhoods to states. Many cities have a department of planning. In some areas, the planning function may reside within the department of community development, the city manager's office, housing, or community services. Some counties and states also have departments of planning.

Planning is also undertaken by nonprofit groups. For example, a nonprofit or community-based organization might develop a housing plan for the homeless or a downtown plan. State and federal agencies will also develop plans for how to spend government money that will encourage development of business or low-income housing, deliver social service programs, or even address tourism.

Planners work most often for government agencies, either as employees or as expert, hired consultants. They may also work for nonprofits, such as coalitions for housing or for developers, architects, and other business people.

Many people participate in the plan, but several groups are required to review and adopt planning activities. Here are the key participants or players:

This sketch of an urban planner was drawn by Alex Barios in San Francisco. In Alex's view, an important part of being a planner is being a communicator.

Planners: Staff or experts who manage the planning process and create the planning information.

Planning Commissioners: The planning commission represents the citizens and reviews the planning efforts and the plans. The commission ensures that the general public has an opportunity to review and comment on the plan.

Other Commissions: In the case of specialized plans, such a heritage tourism plan, some entity or agency, such as local historic preservation commission, may be the review group.

City Council or other legislative body: These bodies have the legal authority to accept or reject the plans. They take responsibility for seeing that the plan is carried out.

Client: Some planning is done for a client. The plan may undergo no more extensive review than by the client who commissioned it. Most likely, the plan will result in projects that go through a review process in which the entities listed above will participate.

Understanding the Community's Problems and Its Resources. The planning process not only looks at what the community members envision, it incorporates an understanding of the problems facing the community. Equally important, it also assesses the community's resources. Through the analytical planning process, planners consider these features in the community:

◆ Physical
◆ Social
◆ Economic

They analyze existing conditions and future trends. Traditionally, planners look most intensely at these issues:

◆ Transportation
◆ Land use
◆ Housing
◆ Recreation and open space
◆ Natural and cultural resources
◆ Community and social services
◆ Population
◆ Economic development

The Political Framework for Planning

Planners help the community members look at the options they have for development and change. Once planners have conducted their analysis, they develop alternatives for solving problems in a coordinated and comprehensive manner. The alternatives are presented to the reviewers and legislative body. These bodies will select among the alternatives, and the pathway they select will guide the future development of the community. The reality of politics dictates that how seriously the various alternatives are considered varies considerably. Most often, leaders will have a particular solution in mind from the start, and the planning effort may be used to justify and show the feasibility of this solution.

Formal plans are presented to community officials, who review, revise, and adopt (or reject) them. The plan provides the instructions for a course of action.

Once the plan is adopted, the planner's job becomes the implementation of the plan, coordinating work among many groups.

The work of planning is to look at the community in the past, present and future tenses.
Noré Winter
Winter & Co.
Boulder, Colorado

CHAPTER 1

CASE STUDIES: LEARNING, LIVING, AND ADVOCACY

There are a variety of reasons to get youth involved in community planning. Educators want to introduce active civic learning into the classroom. Community planners and policymakers reach out for a more inclusive view of their communities by integrating youth concerns. Communities and parents seek an informed atmosphere for citizenship and leadership training. And young people want their aspirations acknowledged in preparing plans for the future.

AGE GROUPS FOR USING CHARRETTES:
5TH GRADE THROUGH ADULT

While young people of any age can participate in planning education projects, the charrette method works best with children who are already at an age where they can work cooperatively, complete a series of different tasks both individually and in a group, and articulate the results of their insights. Therefore, it is unlikely a charrette would work well with children below the 5th grade level.

There is no upper age limit to who can participate in charrettes. Indeed, a charrette that combined youth and senior adults might be among the most exciting a planner or teacher could devise. In planning processes, it is common for planners to separate charrette participants into adult and youth groups. However, Roger Hart, in his insightful book, *Children's Participation: The Theory and Practice of Involving Young Citizens in Community Development and Environmental Care*, advocates strongly for developing youth programs that include adults or that mix young people of different ages.

YOUTH CHARRETTES IN TEACHING

Using charrettes to augment the standard educational curriculum in schools and other educational institutions offers an opportunity to provide a boost to the educational objectives. In a focused effort, it incorporates other professional and community participants and blends learning with active citizenship activities. From elementary students to high school students, special events and charrettes can add value and richness to the classroom experience. For teachers of civics or government, design or art, history or social studies, special events that allow students to focus on a particular place and issue can be a very effective way to make the lesson real.

When using a charrette, the educational objectives will vary from place to place; however, char-

A well-designed charrette taps into young people's interests and talents. In Albuquerque, planners added to the excitement and enjoyment of the event by having students participate in graphic design. In this case they worked on vibrant murals based on prehistoric Mexican art.

rette events offer an occasion for others to get involved in the educational process. Some of the added benefits of conducting charrettes are that students will be mentored by the volunteer participants, as well as exposed to new career opportunities, and introduced to civic role models. Volunteers for these programs can include planners, architects, landscape architects, engineers, politicians, public safety professionals, business people, artists, and elected officials.

In the case studies presented here, some schools shared resources to undertake this type of event. They also took advantage of nonprofit institutions that specialize in augmenting school curriculum. For example, in the New York and San Francisco areas there are Architects-in-the-School programs that focus on environmental design education. In Utah and Indiana, planners conduct Planners Day in Schools programs.

There are many community-based organizations (CBOs) and institutions involved in youth development. These organizations provide ongoing after-school programs that augment classroom activities. They stress citizenship development and cultural enrichment of young people. Many of these organizations emphasize empowerment, which they define as providing knowledge and motivating young people to "take ownership" of projects and communities. They are committed to the belief that youth can help change their communities for the better. In San Francisco, St. Johns Urban Institute illustrates how these organizations use charrettes. The goal is to immerse young people in curriculums that will increase their understanding of their community and create concrete projects that improve neighborhoods for youth and families.

CASE STUDIES

Wherever youth are engaged in a charrette process there is a tremendous opportunity to provide a learning experience. Educators have found the hands-on and experienced-based qualities of a charrette can offer an intensive educational opportunity. This happens in schools, museums, and other community-based organizations that stress enhancing young peoples' communication skills and understanding of urban issues.

Museum-Based Case Studies

Many museums have sponsored workshops. Included in our case study examples are the APA's 1997 Kids' Planning Charrette in San Diego; and Cooper Hewitt Museum, National Design Museum, and the New York Chapter of the American Institute of Architects ongoing "A City of Neighborhoods—Bridging School and Community" program.

The San Diego Kids' Planning Charrette included an environmental walk in which students stopped at preselected locations and recorded observations on their base maps. This exercise led to the development of a plan.

American Planning Association and the San Diego Children's Museum
April 1997

Mass transit in the form of kidmobiles and light industry in the form of a chocolate factory—those were some of the ideas that came out of the charrette to redesign the neighborhood surrounding the San Diego Children's Museum into a kid-friendly neighborhood.

This case study illustrates a strictly educational charrette. With more time devoted to the project, the charrette could easily have been integrated into a planning process. However, the goal in this case was to teach planners how to conduct charrettes, with the students serving as "instructors" on the process.

Absorbed by their task, Zamorano Elementary School students found any convenient surface for drawing their observations of the neighborhood on walking tour maps.

Who

APA members and staff created the charrette. The one-day event brought planners, several teachers and the 5th and 6th grades from the Zamorano Elementary School together for the planning event. In this charrette the roles broke down into: 3 facilitators; 3 staff, 30 planners/kids' assistants, 3 teachers, and 65 students.

Context

The event was held as both an education workshop and a community outreach event as part of the 1997 APA National Planning Conference in San Diego. The event took place in the San Diego Children's Museum, a wonderful, sunny, colorful, and open space in which the students worked in groups at tables. Museum staff provided support in setting up the event.

Goals

◆ Introduce planners to the principles of conducting a charrette with a youth group.
◆ Demonstrate how planning concepts could be made into a problem-solving educational event.
◆ Provide elementary school students a one-day introduction to planning issues and concepts in terms of their own community.
◆ Acquaint teachers in the San Diego school system with an educational enrichment program on city planning.

How

The day had three major segments. The entire event took place between 8:30 a.m. and 4:30 p.m., with the students arriving at 9:30 a.m. and leaving at 2:00 p.m. This was the agenda:

◆ Introduction and orientation for planners
◆ Charrette with students
   Exercise one: cognitive mapping and drawing your neighborhood
   Debriefing

   Exercise two: environmental walk and mapping of museum neighborhood

   Exercise three: neighborhood design game
   Reporting: three big and cool ideas

   Exercise four: designing a kids' charrette in your own community

◆ Debriefing for planners and teachers

The 65 children were broken into eight groups. Kids' assistants—the planners who had registered for the workshop—were assigned to a group throughout the charrette. All three teachers actively participated with the students. The facilitators' role was to explain each of the assignments and to debrief the group after each exercise. Staff assistants oversaw the supplies, snacks, lunches, equipment, and general logistics.

What

The area surrounding the San Diego Children's Museum is in transition. Bounded on one side by the harbor, that boundary is changing from industrial and maritime facilities to convention centers and large resort hotels. To the north, the area is bounded by the historic Main Street and a more recent mall development, Horton Plaza. On the east are low-rise older apartment buildings and small retail businesses and to the west are smaller, industrial buildings. In the last few years the city has attempted to bring more residences into the area and now several expensive, high-rise condominiums exist side-by-side with SROs (Single Residency Occupancy hotels) and low- and moderate-income townhouses. During the months prior to the workshop, other residential features were added to the neighborhood, including a children's park (but not one that allowed for play) and a grocery store.

First the students were asked to think about their own neighborhoods and to draw them. Next they took a preplanned environmental walk using maps of the area. They were asked to stop at several points and make observations about the neighborhood, recording the results with notes on their maps and Polaroid photos. Each group had a camera. Upon returning to the museum, the kids transferred their observations to a larger scale map of the area that showed outlines of buildings and streets. In the next stage, they used precut game pieces and treated a clean base map as the game board. Taking the ideas from their large scale map, they created a three-dimensional model and plan of the neighborhood. In playing the game, they organized it to convey three "big and cool" ideas about how they would design the neighborhood to make it more kid friendly. Each group then reported back to the group at large on their plans, while a facilitator recorded the ideas and organized them into major planning concepts. For example, the kids observed that traffic needed to be rerouted in the neighborhood to make some streets quieter and safer to walk. They also decided there needed to be a better mix of features in the neighborhood, such as more stores and a swimming pool.

Clients

Ideally, the client for this project would have been the Downtown Development Corporation that coordinates the city's involvement in the area. Indeed, the DDC assisted APA in providing information, maps, and photographs. However, as this was strictly an educational event, the ultimate clients were the planners who participated in the program and the teachers from Zamorano Elementary School.

CASE STUDY 2
A CITY OF NEIGHBORHOODS— BRIDGING SCHOOL AND COMMUNITY

A City of Neighborhoods
Fort Greene & Clinton Hill
Spring 1997

BRIDGING

SCHOOL

AND

COMMUNITY

The National Design Museum focuses on a different neighborhood each year in its ongoing program, A City of Neighborhoods. Adults learn about their neighborhood and how to use it as a resource for teaching children about their physical, historic, and social environment.

Cooper Hewitt Museum, National Design Museum, and the NY Chapter of the American Institute of Architects
New York City
Ongoing

Cooper Hewitt, the National Building Museum, which is a branch of the Smithsonian Institution, describes the program this way: A City of Neighborhoods is for educators, architects, and community activists who are interested in working together to integrate community resources across the K-12 curricula.

Who

Cooper Hewitt Museum runs a community exploration program that involves teachers, architects, and community activists. Some segments of the program are also open to the general public. In addition to the museum staff, the program draws upon planners, architects, preservationists, and local community leaders as resources and instructors.

Context

The context is an ongoing program. As "Bridging School and Community," the program is being developed for national audiences in rural, suburban, and urban communities.

Goals

◆ Train teachers to use the physical city as a resource for teaching.

- Encourage the use of primary sources (historic resources) and primary resources (the people engaged in shaping the city) in schoolroom teaching.
- Bring teachers together with advocates of city planning, such as professional architects and planners, in developing programs.
- Provide a forum for community members to explore and discuss their neighborhood's planning issues.

How

The program consists of several elements: public lectures, community-based workshops, and curriculum implementation. Each course focused on one New York City neighborhood. Three one-hour public lectures take place at the museum on Friday evenings. Various speakers discuss architectural history, architecture, and planning issues in the neighborhood.

Three all-day workshops are held on three Saturdays following the lectures given to course participants. These are workshops for teachers, architects, and community activists. "Participants will develop a design vocabulary, explore how neighborhoods change over time, and examine community issues and . . . learn the fundamentals of developing design-based curriculum projects" reads the brochure.

Workshop activities:

Reading historic photographs.
Observing the neighborhood on an environmental walk, with an emphasis on architectural history.
Visiting a museum exhibit on homelessness.

What

The final products often involve architects visiting schools through the "Learning by Design" Committee of the New York Chapter of the AIA.

Client

As an educational program, the clients were the participants—students and adults.

School-Based Case Studies

Teachers are finding the workshop or charrette approach to augmenting traditional classroom instruction a valuable tool. Included in our case study examples are several school-based charrettes including: LEAP/AIA Architects in the Schools Program in the San Francisco Bay Area, George Washington Carver Elementary in San Francisco, and Kramer Junior High School in Washington, D.C.

A City of Neighborhoods
The Bronx:
Melrose Commons
Spring 1998
BRIDGING
SCHOOL
AND
COMMUN

The National Design Museum builds program identity through consistent graphic imagery over the years. Perhaps the most challenging aspect of charrette-based education is maintaining the momentum of the program over time. Often institutional support, such as that offered by a museum, is necessary to keep a program alive.

ARCHITECTS IN THE SCHOOLS PROGRAM

These young people are presenting their model for a sustainable community as part of LEAP's Architects-in-the-Schools program in the San Francisco Bay Area.

LEAP/AIA
San Francisco Bay Area
1984-present

For 13 years the LEAP/AIA Architects in Schools Program has been introducing Bay Area children to the world of architecture and planning. The program pairs professional architects with teachers for eight-week residencies in the school classrooms. Through a series of exercises, projects, and field trips, architects expose children to issues in the built, natural, and cultural environment.

During the 1997-98 school year, architects from Bay Area firms worked with more than 1,300 young people in residencies in 43 elementary school classes. The children who participate in the LEAP/AIA Architects in Schools Program are elementary and middle school students in the San Francisco, Daly City, Marin, Alameda, San Mateo, and Oakland school districts. The students range in age from 8 to 13. Most of the participating schools are public schools. The student participants are from diverse neighborhoods, with a large majority of Asian, Latino, and African descent.

Currently there are 52 architects from the San Francisco Bay Area working in the LEAP/AIA Program. Each architect on the roster is trained within the LEAP program to develop curriculum and work as educators with children. This roster includes a high percentage of African, Latino, and Asian Americans and females. During the course of the residencies, other professionals, such as landscape architects, environmental building consultants, urban planners, and community activists, may be invited to share knowledge and information with the children. Together the architects and students create innovative design proposals for homes, schools, neighborhoods, and communities.

During the past few years, in the LEAP/AIA program, children have grappled with local urban development issues and crafted imaginative proposals for the Bay Bridge, the Presidio Military Base Conversion, Treasure Island, Union Square, Mission Bay, Crissy Field, and more. They have also tackled tough social issues such as homelessness and environmental sustainability.

Architects working on projects with children and youth often say they are "hooked" on it. They say it helps them remember why they love architecture. They can explore ideals about the built environment and community life while sharing the unfettered vibrancy of young peoples' imagination.

Two national institutions have joined forces to examine and document the dynamics of these intense learning experiences: the Carnegie Foundation for the Advancement of Teaching and the American Architectural Foundation. They argue that the methods found in the best design studios—critical thinking, problem solving, teamwork, and integrative learning—can help students draw more sophisticated connections between subjects such as math, science and the arts. Their new report, "Building Connections," outlines ways that the architectural design process can be more thoroughly integrated into the K-12 educational curriculum in the nation's schools. The collaborative supporting LEAP represents more than 30 Bay Area nonprofits, museums, and architectural firms. All are working to create and expand opportunities in design, planning, and civic activism for children and youth. Shirl Buss assisted in developing this case study.

The LEAP program sharpens the visual and verbal communication skills of students through a variety of activities.

Goals

During the 1997-98 school year, with the support of the Marin Community Foundation, the LEAP/AIA program conducted a series of residencies in eight elementary schools on the theme "Parks, Playgrounds and People Movers: Children's Designs for Sustainable Communities."

Architects and teachers planned activities for children to explore issues of sustainability and interconnectedness in the built, cultural, and natural environments. Through a series of smaller participatory mini-activities, the students studied basic ideas such as structure, scale, design, and city planning. They also investigated some of the issues associated with the ecological health of cities at different scales: the home, the neighborhood, the city, and the region. Each class, guided by "their architect," planned, designed, and built a final project on a selected theme of community sustainability.

The goal was to create a context within which the children were able to do the following with their environment: observe it, analyze and critique it, develop proposals to transform it, and build skills to communicate their ideas about it. Many of the children's projects were also on exhibit in various locations throughout the Bay Area.

How

During the 1997-98 school year, architects met with the students for eight weeks, two to three hours per week. To launch the project, the architects and teachers involved consultants from Ecological Design Institute to explore ways in which design education can collaborate with the "green architecture" movement. They reviewed projects throughout the Bay Area, where designers used ecologically sustainable materials and practices such as straw bale walls, solar collectors, water reuse systems, and recycled building materials.

Architects and teachers customized each residency so that architecture and sustainability aug-

Two more participants in the LEAP program admire one another's drawings of the neighborhood.

mented and amplified the academic curriculum. Next, the architects crafted an eight-week lesson plan for each class. The weekly topics complemented other curricular areas, striking a balance between the arts and sciences and a social and political context.

Students saw slide shows (drawings, models, and videos) to stimulate their interest and give them information about the environment. Mini-activities connected various aspects of the design process to their experiences. The children next applied these skills as they explored issues of sustainability during the final project. Presentations for parents, teachers, other students, city officials, or community members culminated the program.

A typical sequence of activities during the residencies followed a scenario similar to this:

WEEK 1: Nature + Architecture
Sources of Inspiration: Slides of animal architecture and vernacular architecture from around the world.
Hands-on Activity: Building habitats using natural materials.

WEEK 2: Materials: Reduce, Reuse, Recycle
Sources of Inspiration: Presentation on how to use recycled materials in architecture (tile made from car windshields, insulation from old blue jeans)
Hands-on Activity: Design a house out of recycled materials.

WEEK 3: Structures: Form and Function
Sources of Inspiration: Slides about "How Buildings Stand Up"
Hands-on Activity: Build structurally sound edifices using different materials and building systems.

WEEK 4: State-of-the-Art Energy Use
Sources of Inspiration: Models of sustainable energy production and conservation
Hands-on Activity: Design a self-contained house using appropriate technologies: solar, wind, water conservation, or biomass.

WEEKS 5-7: Final Project
Sources of Inspiration: Visits by city planners, community activists
Hands-on Activity: Conduct research, photograph sites, work in teams, develop plans, create bubble diagrams, write about and work collaboratively to build model of final project proposal.

WEEK 8 and beyond: Presentations
Present models, writings, diagrams to parents, students, city officials, school board, community activists.

Exhibitions

Some of the students' work was included in an exhibition called "Bridging Communities: Children's Architecture Projects 1997-98" shown during the 1998 AIA National Convention in San Francisco. Others were displayed at open houses at San Rafael City Hall and at Pickleweed Park.

What

"A School in the Year 2050"
Fourth Grade Students
Teacher: Lisa Hanley
Architects: Ann West and Fran Halperin
The Problem: After a minor earthquake in 2050, San Rafael is now an island. The students (now in their 60s and professional artists, educators, builders, and politicians) are to reopen the school for their grandchildren, who are now in 4th grade. Using the old buildings on the site, they design independent systems for heating, power, clean water, food, waste disposal, and transportation. The students break into teams to brainstorm about each system. Next, they collaboratively plan how the systems would relate to each other. Finally, they are to construct a model for a sustainable community on the school site.

"Earth, Air, Water"
Fifth Grade Students
Teacher: Lara Heller
Architect: Shirl Buss
Community Collaborators: Rebecca Coffman, Deirdre Holmes—Ecological Design Institute
The students explored the relationship between built, cultural, and natural environments of a sustainable community. For this project they focused on the quality of the air, water, and land, as well as the transportation systems linking up the various parts of the community. The children planned, designed, and built a model of an ecologically and socially sustainable or healthy environment including: high-density housing nested in beanstalks, a solar/power wind power plant, water purifying fountains, and flying cars.

"The Canals of San Rafael"
Fifth Grade Students
Teacher: Cindy Bradlee
Architects: Anne Laird-Blanton and John Klimek
Community Collaborators: Bruce Race, SPUR (San Francisco Planning and Urban Research Association), Kevin Conger (Landscape Architect-Hargreaves Associates), Lionel Ashcroft (Marin Historical Society)
Because many of the students live in the Canal District, they are aware of the waterways in San

The LEAP students were hard at work drawing maps and building models of their sustainaible communities.

One of the objectives of the LEAP program is to allow young people to express their ideas, not only through verbal presentations, but with maps, drawings, and models.

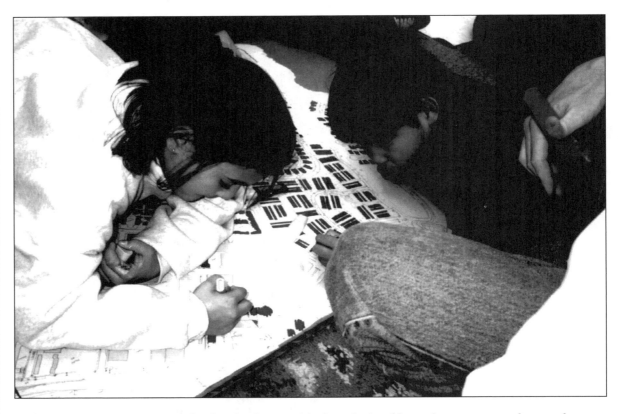

Rafael. They spent many weeks developing a critical analysis of how the areas near the canals work. They took photos of their favorite places, and photos of areas that they felt "didn't work." Using information gleaned from the consultants from EDI and the San Jose Guadalupe Waterway Park, the students developed a proposal for reuse of the canals. Their proposals included bikeways, paths, bridges, public space, more shopping options, and parks. They presented their findings and proposal to the San Rafael City Council and the planning commission.

"Windmills"
Fifth Grade Students
Teacher: Oliver Mitchell
Architects: Aurora Robinson-Baptiste
Engineer: Tom Tormey
Currently the students are building a solar greenhouse and a garden. For this project, after preliminary studies about scale and structure, the students embarked on a project to design and build a bat-

tery-charging windmill. After building small model prototypes and doing an extensive site analysis, the students collaborated to build a full-scale windmill to be located next to the greenhouse.

"Connections"
Fourth, Fifth Grades
Teachers: Barbara Wander, Jason Knighton, Karen Bennasini
Architects: Rich Storek, Tom Laughlin, Jim Leefe

The students in three classes spent the entire residency investigating the idea of connections. They first explored human connections. Using photography, they designed a connection wheel in which students created icons to represent their names and attached them to photos of their faces. Then each student worked with a partner, someone with whom they usually did not work. Together they created a connecting person who was inserted between their respective photos. This connecting person was constructed with composite photos of each partner and composite icons representing their names joined together. They then went on to explore connections between different building elements, using tetrahedrons for construction. Finally they built a community emphasizing the connections between the form and function of all of the buildings.

Clients

These are educational programs and so the students, teachers, and school administrators are the clients.

George Washington Carver 4th and 5th graders designed their own courtyard garden. Along the way they met experts in gardening, urban planning, and others who answered questions and allowed them to test and improve their skills.

Carver Elementary
San Francisco, California
1997-98

A creative approach to education at George Washington Carver has resulted in a very energetic student council. At Carver, student candidates campaign for positions, write press releases, and hold press interviews to gain support from fellow students. The council insists that students register to vote in elections. Carver Elementary, located in the Bayshore/Hunters Point community, is one of San Francisco's lowest income neighborhoods. Historically,

CASE STUDY 4

GEORGE
WASHINGTON
CARVER
ELEMENTARY
GARDEN
PROJECT

the school has attracted outside resources to supplement the academic program. Each new project becomes an extension of the classroom, teaching students to become active citizens.

In 1998, the student council and administration initiated a school garden project that was planned through a three-step charrette and workshop process.

Who

Throughout the one-month planning process, the student council acted as the advisory committee to George Washington Carver faculty and outside adult volunteers. The volunteer planners met with the council and other students to gather information for the plans. Twice each week, the planner volunteers conducted a workshop-style session with students on topics identified by the students as their learning and advocacy objectives for the project.

The volunteer planners were members of San Francisco Planning and Urban Research Association's (SPUR's) youth program. They contracted with a Coro Foundation Fellow to serve as project manager. The project was funded with a grant from Pacific Gas and Electric Company (PG&E). Throughout the process SPUR solicited expert volunteers from around the community to assist in the planning effort.

Context

The month-long planning process for the gardens took place during the school's spring session. For security reasons, the garden project focused on the building courtyards. The courtyards were paved residual spaces, oddly shaped and with variable sunlight. The students faced a variety of technical and logistical problems, including a lack of funding to implement their plans. Therefore, the planning process required the students to network with other schools with successful gardens to gain knowledge and advocate for funding.

Goals

The students identified three goals for the garden planning and construction and planting.

◆ The project must include an opportunity to apply basic math skills. Students had to measure and draw the oddly shaped spaces.
◆ The project must include a science component. Students learned about plants.
◆ The project must include a health component. The students increased their knowledge of diet and healthy eating habits.

How

The program was designed as a three-step process: discovery, planning, and doing. As students worked on their plan, faculty and volunteer planners met with a number of other organizations and individuals to gain knowledge that would inform the students' planning program. This is the outline for the program.

Step 1: Discovery

Session 1 – Drawing the courtyards
Session 2 – What is a successful garden? Presentation by urban gardener
Session 3 – How do you design a garden? Presentation by landscape architect
Session 4 – What is a healthy garden? What should we grow? Presentation by a dietitian

Step 2: Planning

Session 1 – Developing Garden Planning Teams
Session 2 – Making a Garden Calendar

Step 3: Doing

Session 1 – Making a Garden Book
Session 2 – Writing Letters Requesting Funding
Session 3 – Sponsoring a Community Event

What

Students outlined the overall planning approach. They helped establish the goals for the garden project, picked the experts that could help teach them to make the garden successful, networked with students at other schools, participated in the hands-on garden design, and advocated for the funding for construction.

Besides learning about an overall process, the students had the opportunity to participate in several workshop-style sessions. The major charrette session was developing the Garden Planning Teams. In this charrette, students prepared a garden plan layout and planting plan. The Garden Planning Teams consisted of five students who used their growing calendar, a selection of plants, the maps of the courtyards, and pieces of cut cardboard to plan the gardens. The students answered three questions while designing their gardens:

1. What plants will be planted and what time of year?
2. Where in the garden will they be planted?
3. How will the selected plants be maintained?

These girls at George Washington Carver did not mind having their projects documented, as long as they were part of the documentation.

The students spent two hours building a scale model of their proposals, and then presented their models, drawings, and plant list to the rest of the teams. They discussed what was similar about the proposals and negotiated a consensus plan formed from all the teams' plans.

Clients

The client/customer for planner volunteers at George Washington Carver Elementary was initially the school administration, but evolved to become the student council. The council is primarily made up of 4th and 5th grade students, who discuss and analyze important issues for the school. The council decided that the garden project could represent an important learning opportunity. They became the promoters of the project and communicated with other students, faculty, parents, and other allied organizations.

Kramer Junior High School
Washington, D.C.
1988-present

This project integrated a neighborhood awareness program with an ongoing planning process. Two distinctive features of the program were the high level of commitment on the part of the school and recruitment of several outside groups in the educational program.

In spring 1992, planners under the auspices of the APA Planners Day in School program visited the school and conducted morning-long sessions on planning. Some sessions focused on city building exercises and one focused on a transportation problem confronting students walking to the Kramer school. This latter session was conducted by planners from the Washington, D.C., planning department. These visiting planners exposed students to careers in planning. Marya Morris wrote about this project in the March 1993 issue of *Planning*, when the project won the APA Public Education Award.

Bill Washburn and Al Dobbins of the Washington, D.C., planning office presented students at Kramer Middle School with the challenge of planning a safer walk to school.

Who

In 1988, Kramer Junior High School principal Zovolia Willis created the idea of a neighborhood planning project for her students. She recruited local universities, the district's board of education, and a neighborhood group, Anacostia Coordinating Council, to participate in the program.

Context
Kramer Junior High School is located in the Anacostia neighborhood of Washington, D.C. This historic black neighborhood has a long history of community involvement by the residents and a rich history for the students to explore. However, the school has limited financial resources, and the volunteer assistance by the universities and the coordinating council became vital to the success of the program.

Goals
- Give students a sense of history and community
- Demonstrate that youth can make changes to improve their neighborhood
- Develop a model that could be adopted throughout the city school system

How
A maximum of 10 hours a week are devoted to the project. During the first semester, 9th grade students in civics class study basic planning skills such as map making and research methods. This is followed in the second semester by an analysis of a particular project led by a visiting planner.

What
In 1991-92 the visiting planner was Margaret O'Bryon, AICP, of George Washington University's Institute for Urban Development Research. O'Bryon chose the redevelopment of a parking lot on Martin Luther King, Jr. Avenue as the project for the classes.

The project team was planning in 1992 to prepare a curriculum for use by other teachers. They were also exploring the possibility of making Kramer a magnet school in neighborhood planning.

Client
The owner of the parking lot was presented with a redevelopment plan by the students.

Community-Based Organizations
Youth advocates in community-based organizations have been using charrettes to empower young people to articulate their own agenda. We have included a case study on how one of these organizations has been using charrettes as an integral part of their training and youth advocacy program.

St. Johns summer program students participated in mapping their neighborhood. They colored maps and took Polaroid photographs of the area to help communicate what they identified as critical issues.

CASE STUDY 6
ST. JOHNS URBAN INSTITUTE

Mission District
San Francisco
1995-present

The Mission District in San Francisco is becoming an increasingly kid-friendly place due to the efforts of Mission youth and the staff of St. Johns Educational Threshold Center (SJETC). Termed the "Devil's Quadrangle" by the San Francisco Police Department, the improvement of the 16th and Mission Street neighborhood has become the project of young people from the ages from 8 to 18.

SJETC created the St. Johns Urban Institute in the summer of 1995 and has demonstrated the power of youth in defining issues important to them, as well as doing something about it. Since 1995, St. Johns Urban Institute has used planning charrettes/workshops as an integral part of the learning and planning process. As a result, the youth at St. Johns have attracted over $500,000 for building a new park in the Inner Mission, created the Safe Streets program by working with merchants to allow children to seek safety in local businesses, and invented the Block by Block effort.

Who

The St. Johns Urban Institute's mission is to provide an after-school and summer learning program. The program supports young men and women in developing initiatives that emphasize social improvement and educational opportunities in the neighborhood. Staff and volunteers use creative arts including poetry, drawing, models/sculpture, and theater to encourage young people to express their vision of a youth-friendly environment.

Context

The Inner Mission District in San Francisco is a culturally diverse community with a large Hispanic population. St. Johns Urban Institute has focused its efforts on the 16th and Mission area that includes a commercial district, a Bay Area Rapid Transit station, and nearby moderate- to high-density residential areas. There is a high incidence of gang violence, drugs, and homelessness in the Inner Mission.

Goals

St. Johns's overall goal is for young people to become full-fledged partners in the community's redevelopment. The charrettes and associated educational programs focus on:

◆ Citizenship development
◆ Academic excellence
◆ Ethical development
◆ Giving young people the resources to shape their own environment

How

Young men and women participate as planning teams in mapping and making proposals for the neighborhood. Working out of a local middle school, they walk the area, make notes, and provide a summary of problems facing the neighborhood. Next, they define the issues and potential opportunities for making the Mission a better place for kids. They work in groups using maps, and their work includes art projects and street improvement projects.

St. Johns Urban Institute's overall approach uses various types of charrette-style exercises in three stages of ongoing planning activities:

Stage One: Mapping the Neighborhood and Community
Exercise One: My Neighborhood – Drawing and writing about the neighborhood
Exercise Two: Community Brainstorm – Relationships in the ideal community
Exercise Three: Visioning – Making banners of the ideal community
Exercise Four: Neighborhood Assessment – Neighborhood land uses
Exercise Five: Neighborhood Brainstorm – What is missing from the neighborhood?

St. Johns students presented their projects to classmates. Stand-up presentations help young people get over their nervousness in presenting their ideas, yet still retain some of the laughter and fun of the project.

After presenting their neighborhood maps, the St. Johns students commented on how many of them felt unsafe. As a result, the students and teachers developed the "Block by Block" program. The program includes the Safe Streets effort and other improvements that won the support of local merchants.

Exercise Six: Youth Goals and Values for Community Development – Writing and acting in skits
Exercise Seven: Needs and Wants – Making lists and connecting wants with needs

Stage Two: Assessing Youth Priorities
Exercise Eight: Our Own Private Space – Creating a model and writing about it
Exercise Nine: Designing a Community Beacon – Planning a Beacon Teen and Family Center
Exercise Ten: Designing a Community with Sand – Participating in competition

Stage Three: Taking Action
Exercise Eleven: Quick Calls in Our Neighborhood – Surveying street corners for safety, making a
    summary map, presenting the map to board of supervisors, working with local businesses
Exercise Twelve: Visiting City Hall - Presenting letters to Mission Task Force
Exercise Thirteen: Advocating Ideas I – Preparing letters to the mayor
Exercise Fourteen: Advocating Ideas II – Preparing letters to the BART board of directors

All these exercises are part of a coordinated art, language, and citizenship/civics program. Teachers, staff, and volunteer planners facilitate exercises that support the youths' advocacy objectives.

Throughout the process, young people continue to refine their understanding of the neighborhood, express their own priorities, and advocate for and implement their positions. The results of their efforts to date include:

◆ Kid Power – Workshops by Kids for Adults
◆ Quick Calls/Safer Streets – Safe havens for youth in local businesses
◆ The Parks Initiative – Have earmarked over $500,000 for a new park

What
For the charrette, the process featured two types of mapping.

This first exercise is called cognitive mapping. By this, we mean that youth are drawing what they already know and they draw from their memory, their perceptions, and their ideas. This exercise allowed them to express their understanding of their own neighborhoods. These resulted in a wide range of drawings—from a picture of their own houses, to a full neighborhood map of streets and landmarks. The maps were also used to express the ideal future in visioning-type workshops.

Inventory mapping included actual land-use surveys, crime surveys, and photographs of favorite buildings and streets (in a sense, maps that represent an agreed upon representation of an area). In a recent exercise, the participants were divided into three teams that surveyed the ingredients of Mission Street/16th Street Places—activities, spaces, and pathways. One team—the activities team—looked at land use. Another—the space team—looked at buildings, streets, landscaping, and open space. The third—the pathways team—recorded where people walked, busy intersections, and transit stops. All three teams recorded their findings on maps and with photographs.

The creative product derived from these surveys and the young peoples' ideas was an "installation" at the St. Johns storefront gallery. The installations have included models of future buildings and places, paintings, and most recently, furniture.

Clients

For organizations like St. Johns, the organization is the client. St. Johns is committed to an ongoing and increasing presence for youth in their communities, so an overall plan that employs a variety of interactive tools is best. Active citizenship for youth develops communication skills and increases young participants' understanding of what makes the community tick. This happens simultaneously with their advocacy activities. The second clients were the volunteer planners that participated with St. Johns staff. They were rewarded by their contribution to an outstanding existing program. Their work helps the ongoing work of this youth advocacy organization.

YOUTH ADVOCATES

In many communities, planners, task forces, and advisory commissions are turning to partnerships with community-based organizations (CBOs) that provide youth programs and access to families. The CBOs provide a venue and structured environment for young people to participate in a planning effort.

One of the mandates in many contemporary federal government programs is for communities to provide extensive community participation. Empowerment Zones, Brownfields Act, ISTEA (Intermodal Surface Transportation Efficiency Act), and HUD (Housing and Urban Development) reinvestment programs require public participation. Some communities are emphasizing young persons' perspectives in finding solutions for planning related to these types of programs. HUD has funded reconstruction of housing and in the process included workshops with neighborhood young people. These events were cosponsored by a local Boy's and Girls' Club. In these communities, young people were expected to take a vested interest in the plans and were viewed as important stakeholders in the planning process.

Community planners are charged with designing public outreach and community participation efforts that stress inclusion of a broad range of community representatives. In many communities, planners and elected officials are reaching out to young people and work with community-based organizations, schools, churches, and other organizations as partners.

As never before, community planning is including a broader spectrum of citizens, organizations, and special interest groups. A handful of established planning processes, such as comprehensive

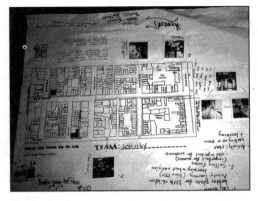

The teams' final project maps and presentations focused on three required elements: the space-design of the street; paths, circulation, and transit; and land use and street activities.

The projects that developed out of the St. Johns charrette program made everyone more aware of young people, their needs, and the contribution they could make to creating a safer environment.

plan updates, incorporate young people. Case studies seven and eight show how the City of Albuquerque, New Mexico, and Lemon Grove, California, engaged young people in policy planning efforts.

Albuquerque youth gathered under the most appropriate heading for a celebratory picture of their Youth Recreational Needs Assessment project.

Consensus Planning, Inc. and the Albuquerque Cultural and Recreation Services Department
Albuquerque, New Mexico
1997

Young people are more aware of bureaucratic shortcomings than city officials may think. The Albuquerque youth recreation needs assessment made that vividly clear to planners and city officials. City Councilor Adele Hundley observed that "one of the things that's lacking in planning is going into the schools and asking students what they need." Participating in the Washington Middle School meeting, she found herself impressed by the students' interest and appreciation of being listened to by planners and politicians.

This case study illustrates how a planning process is linked directly to implementation, increasing the faith of young people in the efficacy of planning. In addition, the planners selected a highly focused planning issue, rather than a broad general plan process, and so allowed for more immediate implementation. A third hallmark of this program was the collaboration of several agencies dealing with youth, which, again, helped increase the implementation of the planning and improved the coordination of services. Perhaps most telling about the power of youth involvement is that the adults heard students identify problems they themselves did not expect to address in this process. The project won an APA national award for special projects in 1998.

Who

Consensus Planning, Inc., a private consulting firm, working for the City of Albuquerque's Cultural and Recreation Services Department, created an event that incorporated middle school students into a critical phase of a planning process—the needs assessment.

In addition to the 600 youth who participated, staff from seven city departments concerned with youth or recreation joined in the effort. Project manager Barbara Baca of the Cultural and Recreation Services Department reflected that it provided a great opportunity for all the youth services people in the city to work together and interact, from police to social services staff.

Context

The Cultural and Recreation Services Department decided to undertake a collaborative planning process in assessing recreation services for youth in the city.

Goals

◆ Learn what students were doing for recreation.
◆ Learn what students wanted for recreation.
◆ Learn what students saw as obstacles to using city recreation programs.
◆ Involve middle school students in planning.
◆ Provide middle school students with a civics lesson.

How

Middle school-aged youth had never before participated in city planning efforts. Therefore, one school from each of the community planning areas within the city was selected for the survey. Next, Pizza Hut and Pepsico joined the effort as caterers for after-school recreational planning parties. At these parties, facilitators conducted the recreational needs survey. Designed as a qualitative survey, the assessment had three questions: What did you do last summer? What do you like to do after school? What programs and services are needed by middle school youth?

What

Clay Campbell, AICP, of Consensus Planning, Inc. observed that students had a remarkable level of awareness of the issues. The survey showed that city youth services needed much better coordination. Second, students reported that middle schools can serve as centers for community-based planning and recreation. Three, like many special population groups, students find inadequate transportation a hindrance to using city programs and facilities. Four, youth use private facilities and programs frequently and this insight alerted planners to the potential of private-public partnerships in meeting youth recreation needs.

Client

City Councilor Adele Hundley and her colleagues were the ultimate clients. They attended the parties and addressed the participants about the value of their participation and the ways in which their ideas would be assessed and implemented. In fact, the needs were so clearly identified that a local bank that learned of the assessment came forward as a sponsor for the implementation program. With the bank's support, during the summer of '97 the CRSD held six Fabulous Fridays at six schools in which a full range of recreational activities were made available to local students for a day. Baca hopes to expand summer recreation programs in subsequent summers to make recreation more geographically accessible to middle school-aged youth.

CASE·STUDY 8
LEMON GROVE KIDS' ELEMENT

The Lemon Grove project resulted in a published plan called the Kids Element; *it was featured on the cover of the American Planning Association's* Resources *newsletter.*

City of Lemon Grove and Lettieri-McIntyre and Associates
Lemon Grove, California
1995-96

Houses should be built over stores so that shopping is easy. The fifth graders in Lemon Grove believe that planning can make life and work easier and safer and they explained to their city officials how it could be done.

In this case study, the planners used an approach that is similar to the program called Box City created by the Center for Understanding the Built Environment. C.U.B.E. sells a complete pre-packaged kit, but the approach is so widespread and popular today that many planners and architects have adapted the concept of the program to their own educational programs, creating their own kits in the process. Where this case study project takes a step beyond a hypothetical exercise into a charrette is in the creation of a mini-plan, called the Kids Element. This project was described by Joan N. Isaacson, AICP, in the Winter 1996 issue of *Resources* newsletter.

Who

Lettieri-McIntyre and Associates, serving as the city's planning consultants, developed a participatory planning program with a class of 5th graders.

Context

The city was updating its comprehensive general plan and decided to expand the level of citizen participation by including youth in the process. A planning consulting firm created the project and carried it out on behalf of city officials.

Goals

◆ Involve students in the planning process to help increase their parents' awareness of the general plan update.
◆ Teach students basic planning concepts.
◆ Solicit ideas from students about how to improve their community.
◆ Increase the range of people who participate in the important planning processes.
◆ Develop an engaging but relatively low-cost project.

How

The consultants held three sessions. Each took place on a separate day and involved several hours of class time. In the first session, planners introduced students to general concepts of planning. Following this, the students constructed various types of buildings needed in a city. Some participants pooled their resources to build condos, entertainment centers, and malls.

A second session focused on types of land use. Students designed their ideal city using the cardboard box buildings they had created in session one. The planners prepared a city grid mat on which the students placed their buildings. As each building was laid down, the planners engaged the students in a discussion of where buildings should be placed and why in terms of zoning and land-use principles.

In the third session, the class discussed their likes and dislikes about their own town. Dividing the class in two, the planners had each group develop a guide on how to make Lemon Grove a better place to live. The planners created specific areas for them to focus on, including: housing and neighborhoods, public buildings, stores and commercial areas, office and factories, and transportation.

Reinforcing the lessons in class were the assignments carried out at home. Students worked with their parents to explore aspects of the city.

What

The 5th graders summarized their findings for the planners, who then wrote a Kids Element for the general plan. In the formal deliberation of general plan by the citizens' committee and the city council, the students presented the Kids Element.

Client

The city officials—council members and citizens committee members—were the client for the program.

CITIZENSHIP AND LEADERSHIP TRAINING

For teens, charrettes can become an integral part of an active civic studies program where they learn by exploring real issues in their communities. Young people can begin to gain a working understanding about local government and how their actions can effect decisions. The ninth case study includes culturally diverse Washington High School and its Healthy Start Program.

Washington High School Healthy Start San Francisco 1996-97

In the Richmond District in San Francisco, high school students have actively pursued the question: "What is a citizen?" Students and faculty advisers embarked on a community visioning and advocacy program that dealt with a wide spectrum of urban planning and social issues from the perspective of youth and families.

In the program at Washington High School, students defined their issues and facilitated their own community summit.

Parents and other community members were drawn into a dialogue about what can be done to improve the quality of life in their ethnically and economically diverse community.

The program used a student-based participation model of planning teams. The process involved a series of workshop sessions and youth summits.

Who

George Washington High School is a Beacon School. Recently, it obtained a $40,000 Healthy Start grant that allows students and their community partners to identify a specific need, a vision for addressing that need, and a scope for a project that is based on active citizenship. The initial classroom-based efforts in 1996 involved 40 students acting as planners. These students worked with professional planner volunteers from the San Francisco Planning and Urban Research Association (SPUR) to develop a scope for their project. SPUR's interactive student- and community-based process helped the young people understand the issues facing the community. Further, during the project they identified opportunities to improve the Richmond District for youth and families.

The Healthy Start effort resulted in the Washington Community Summit. For this event, the students became the managers, facilitators, artists, and documenters of a planning process. Initially, the summit involved other students, and then expanded to include the larger community.

Context

The Richmond District is a four-square-mile area of moderately dense residential neighborhoods focused around commercial streets filled with local businesses. The district is a culturally and economically diverse area in northwestern San Francisco. The community has a growing number of Chinese, Southeast Asian, and Eastern European families. Many youth are second generation citizens finding their way through a "dual" cultural community, one in which immigrant residents may have not been politically active on community issues.

The Washington Community Summit focused on issues in neighborhoods around the high school.

Goals

The purpose of the summit was to share with the community the results of neighborhood mapping and assessment activities conducted by students. Everyone was invited to share his or her perceptions and offer suggestions as to how the community can best provide for the total well-being of students and their families.

The Washington Community Summit had three overall objectives:

◆ Empower students, families, and the community by learning from each other.
◆ Collectively find common ground between the students' concerns and the concerns of their families and the community.
◆ Decide what top three actions to take as a community.

How

The Washington Community Summit had five steps. Accomplishing these steps took four months.

Step 1. Establishing the Ground Rules

At the first meeting, the group established basic ground rules. They agreed the process was going to be run and facilitated by students. (Adults would have to raise their hands and ask permission the speak during meetings and working sessions.)

Step 2. Understanding the Issues

Initially, the students did several cognitive mapping exercises to express their views on the positive and negative issues facing the Richmond District from a youth's perspective. The students selected interest areas and did original research including on-the-street interviews, talking to community leaders, conducting surveys, mapping, and developing demographic summaries.

Step 3. Preparing for the Summit

Working with a professional facilitator, students learned the basics of facilitation. With the issues and messages established, the student planners prepared an agenda for a three-part summit: present the student planners' research findings, facilitate focus group workshops, and share focus group recommendations.

Step 4. Facilitating the Summit

During the summit, the students took the lead in playing the master of ceremonies role, facilitating, and documenting the results.

Step 5. Recording the Results

The research leading to the summit and summit itself was documented and summarized by the student planners. This included a video, photographs, and written results.

What

The overall process involved a charrette-style session with the students that took place at the SPUR office conference space. The results were used to scope the types of research and community outreach that was needed to prepare for the summit. The agenda for the working session answered three questions from the students' perspective:

◆ What are the top three issues?
◆ What are the top three priorities?
◆ Who should the students reach out to in the process?

The student planners were asked to do three exercises.

Exercise 1. Mapping the issues

The students were asked to draw a map of their neighborhood. On the map, they had to list the top three issues. Next, the students gathered into five-person planning teams and made a list of the top issues. The teams presented their findings back to the whole group.

Exercise 2. Mapping what's missing

During this phase, the students had to add to their maps what they felt was missing from their neighborhood.

Exercise 3. List who has to be involved to be successful

Finally, the students discussed and listed who they need to reach out to in the community. They defined who the stakeholders were, and who would work with them to help address the issues and accomplish their objectives.

The materials used for the working session were kept simple—only flip chart paper and markers were required.

Clients

The clients for this project were students from the Richmond and other neighborhoods that attend George Washington High School.

Students presented their own ideas in the Washington High School summit, and recorded the comments and the observations of other participants.

CHAPTER 2

GETTING READY FOR WORKSHOPS AND CHARRETTES

LEARNING OBJECTIVES

Young people get more out of a planning and advocacy effort if they participate in running the show. When possible, they should identify the issues that are important to them, do their own research, explore problems and solutions, and present the results. Our jobs as planners and educators is to create an environment where their efforts are optimized. This means helping map out the overall process, dealing with the logistical requirements for events, and making sure the process is inclusive.

There will be times when you will not have the time to institute a fully democratic process at each step of the program. To save time, you may decide to prepare research materials or select the area, such as the neighborhood, to focus on. That is fine, as long as the charrette allows for active and democratic participation at several steps along the way. If the program is too rigidly structured and if adults participate with too heavy a hand, young people will "smell a rat," and be less eager to participate.

For planners there may be an overwhelming temptation to direct students to the "good" planning solution. Beware! You are not participating in the charrette as the consulting expert, but as a facilitator and "kids' assistant."

As the facilitator or charrette leader, you need to be clear about what your goals are for the charrette as well. In some cases, you may use the charrette as a "hook" to grab parents' attention and get them more deeply involved in a planning process. In other cases, you may be using the charrette as a purely educational experience limited to a one-time event. In the case of the American Planning Association, we conduct charrettes to teach planners techniques for working with children or for conducting charrettes. Know what you are doing and why before you start, and make certain you communicate your goals.

IDENTIFYING THE PLANNING ISSUES

A planner recently observed that planning issues are all around us, but often people do not recognize them as planning issues. To that we add, "Precisely." The charrette, therefore, is an important means of creating awareness of why community problems and debates can be addressed through good planning.

A charrette process and organization should be structured so that it touches on these key plan-

Chia Wan, China Program Specialist at the Children's Musuem of Boston, leads planners on an environment walk. The planners were learning to develop youth education programs and started by observing the characteristics and institutions that define Chinatown.

Selecting a planning topic may involve nothing more than a walk or drive though the community to see what's on residents' minds. This topic would allow students to explore varying points of view, as well as the emotions that sometimes accompany planning issues.

ning questions, addresses young participants' issues, and provides a way for youth to gain a better understanding of their community.

Identifying the Issues Ahead of Time

If your time with the youth is limited, say only a few hours on one day, you may wish to pre-select the problems or issues your charrette will address. You have many options for selecting your charrette study problem.

Canvas the Local Issues and Select a Problem. Here are some tips on how to start. Read the newspaper. Visit a city council or planning commission meeting, the local historic preservation commission, or a local parks board or environmental group, such as a Nature Conservancy chapter. Visit with the city planning department staff. Any of these sources should be able to provide you with an issue that is current, pressing, and interesting. If you work in a planning department or are a consultant in the community, you will have no end of possible problems or issues to choose from.

Geography will also determine your issues and problem. In working with the San Diego Children's Museum, we selected the neighborhood surrounding the museum for three reasons: many planning initiatives were going on in the area; the district was attempting to become a residential and mixed-use neighborhood; and it was convenient in terms of designing a four-hour charrette—the problem was right at hand. In the Anacostia-Kramer School project, the teachers selected the immediate neighborhood to help increase the students' awareness of their own surroundings and increase a sense of personal history and identity. Neighborhoods have an intimate scale and are therefore more comprehensible and familiar for youth. From a planner's perspective, they are also complex enough to allow for excellent planning analysis. However, a specific site can work as well.

Identifying Your Client or Sponsor. In selecting a charrette issue, you need to think about who is the audience for the solution to the problem. Most often the client is the person or agency that can effect the changes the charrette participants are suggesting be made. While most often the client is someone with resources or authority to make changes, in other cases, the client may be someone the group believes needs to be informed or who will benefit from its work. For example, in the case of a planning charrette that focuses on the elderly, the client might be a special interest group of elderly citizens, i.e. the local chapter of the American Association of Retired People or the residents of an elderly housing complex.

Youth Selecting Their Issue

Charrette participants can also select their own issue. You will need to allow more time for this approach. A good way to begin an open brainstorming session on problem identification is to use the day's newspaper. Have young people read several articles that relate to community problems and then list the topics on the board. Start with a general discussion. "Are these problems important? Do they affect your life? Are there other problems?"

Next, you need to set boundaries for the discussion to help the young people focus. When working with younger children, selecting a familiar territory will help them understand the physical dimension of the charrette. Also, for convenience sake, you may wish to select a geographical area that is close enough for the young people to visit easily.

If many issues emerge, list them on the board or flip chart. The participants can then vote on which one(s) they want to work on for the charrette. As facilitator, you can help shape the issue into a specific problem that the young people can address. As an example, if young people say the town is boring, ask them to be more specific and solicit ideas on what they like to do or would like to do. Or, if they say they are afraid of violence, ask more specifically where they are most afraid. Ask who they are afraid of and in what circumstances.

The participants should have no difficulty identifying a wide variety of challenging planning problems. Allowing the participants to select which problem to focus on allows them to take the first step in the civic participation process and develop a sense of ownership.

How to Select a Planning Issue

We defined *planning issue* in Chapter One. Now here are some ideas for selecting an issue and framing it for the charrette. Contemporary life should provide you with more than enough to choose from.

NIMBYs: Give the community a necessary, but undesirable project or NIMBY (Not in My Backyard), such as a trash incinerator.

Neighborhoods: Make a neighborhood more kid-friendly by improving safety and children's play and recreation.

Parks and greenways: Create a greenway system (parks, nature areas, and other "green" areas) that kids would use for recreation and getting to and from school.

Elderly: Redesign a neighborhood to make it serve the needs of elderly residents better.

Safe and efficient travel: Examine travel to the grocery store or to school and redesign it to make it more efficient and safe.

Recreation: Create new play areas in older parks that match current recreational sports and activities.

Pollution: Explore the causes of pollution in a pond or wetland and examine what can be done to clean up the site.

Rehabilitating old buildings: Find new uses and design solutions for outdated and unused buildings such as schools, warehouses, industrial buildings, or stores.

Historic preservation: Explore and analyze architecture and the built environment to decide what to preserve and how to preserve it.

The heart of the community: Identify the place that represents the center or the heart of the community for young people. Create a plan to enhance or preserve that heart.

Tips for Selecting Youth Planning Issues

Help the young participants by offering some general approaches to issues. Geography, age, and topic are three ways of thinking about planning issues.

◆ A geographical area:
 neighborhood
 commercial street
 the area around the school
 the areas where young people
  play around their home
 areas that are good for farming,
  but are used for housing

◆ A set of age-specific issues:
 places for young people to hang out
 comfortable places for young
  children and mothers in parks
 places to stay for homeless youth
 the safety of an elderly person's
  walk to the grocery store
 easy transportation for mother
 and father to go to work

◆ Topics or themes:
 transportation
 homelessness
 improving the environment
 maintaining farmland in the county

Marina Neighborhood is located south of Downtown San Diego's Business District. The Centre City Community Plan calls for this area to become a residential mixed use neighborhood.

Providing a graphic to illustrate the project area or the problem is helpful in defining the planning topic. Here the charrette leader circled the project area on an aerial photo and placed it in the workbook for the charrette.

Youth Participants Identifying Their Client

As mentioned previously, you need a client or sponsor for the recommended solutions to the problem. Ideally, you will incorporate the client into the early stages of the charrette. As an adult, part of your task will be to help young people see how the civic process takes place. You will have the best idea of who the client should be, but an open-ended discussion with youth participants on this point would also be helpful for them. For example, many of them may not know the role a city council plays in making decisions about their community. Depending on the project, there may be different or multiple clients.

As part of their growing awareness of the civic process, youth participants will need to learn:

◆ Who the client is.
◆ What kind of decision the client can make about the problem.
◆ What the client needs to know about the problem.
◆ How best to communicate the results of the charrette to the client.
◆ What resources the client has for addressing the problem.

In this way, young people begin to understand some of the process of how the community solves its problems. See the case study on the Albuquerque Youth Assessment Program in Chapter 1 for an example of how to integrate the clients into the program.

When possible, the client should attend some of the early steps in the charrette. The client can help provide information for the project research and identify how the final solution to the problem should be presented (an oral presentation, a written report, a scale model exhibit, attendance at a client's meeting, etc.). You and your participants may decide that there are several appropriate clients.

Clients can be any number of groups, such as:

◆ The planning department and the planning commission
◆ Downtown development or business group
◆ A city agency such as the parks or housing department or the transit authority
◆ A funder, such as Civic League
◆ A special interest group such as the elderly, a Friends of the Parks group, or the Boy's and Girl's Club
◆ Property owners
◆ Principal of the school and the school board
◆ Neighborhood organization
◆ Parents

WORKSHOP AND CHARRETTE LOGISTICS

Research

Research allows students to enter on a course of discovery. Mapping of the research data allows participants to look for patterns of issues and gain a better understanding about the cause and effect.

As the charrette leader, you will need to do some research ahead of time. You will collect background information that allows you to assess the situation. You will also need to know what materials are available for use in the charrette. In a more lengthy charrette program, you may have the students collect the research data themselves. If you use that option you will have to give them some clues as to where to look. Don't forget that getting around to various agencies and libraries may simply be too difficult for the young people if they don't have someone to chauffeur them from site to site.

Among the types of information you and the participants will collect are:

◆ Newspaper articles (library or newspaper office)
◆ Land-use maps (planning department)

Research materials should include basics such as maps, plans, photographs, reports, and demographic information.

The charrette does not always need to be in a school. Planners can work with Girl Scout troops, after school programs, or in museum settings.

◆ Zoning maps (planning or zoning department)
◆ Building footprint and street maps (planning or engineering department)
◆ Photographs of the buildings, streetscapes, or landscapes (planning department, chamber of commerce, historic preservation group, historical society)
◆ Planning reports or plans (planning department, mayor's office)
◆ Interviews of city officials, residents and interested people (as defined by participants)
◆ Population statistics (planning department, library, or mayor's office)
◆ Articles or books related to the topic (library or planning department)

Exercises, which are discussed in Chapter 3, will also serve as a research methodology.

Logistics

In preparing for a charrette you will have to determine when to start planning, understand who will participate, assign roles for the charrette helpers, assess your equipment needs, consider the type of space to hold the event in, and decide what food or meals need to be arranged. To make certain you use your time with young people for education and not preparation, you will need to have logistics well in hand when the charrette begins. "Flying by the seat of your pants" is highly overrated.

Planning and Lead Time. The charrette can be as brief as a half-day or as lengthy as several weeks. If you are working within a school setting, obviously you will need to coordinate with the school before setting the schedule. You need to know exactly how much time you have and how the students' day is arranged. If you are a planner, remember that teachers' schedules are very crowded, so be flexible. Also, the planner and teacher should work closely to make certain the time allotted is appropriate for the charrette.

As illustrated in the case studies in Chapter 1, the charrette need not be done within the school setting. Planners can work with a Girl or Boy Scout troop or an education program at a museum. When working with museums or extracurricular youth programs, you still need to discuss the schedule carefully with the officials of these programs. Undoubtedly, when working with a museum, you will work with the museum education staff, which we highly recommend. Again, be flexible and expect to adapt your program to the environment in which you are working.

We recommend three months for planning the charrette. For those with experience and well-honed techniques, the lead time can be much less, but seldom ever less than three weeks.

Understanding Your Participants. Once you have found a school, a group of teachers (if you are a planner), a planner (if you are a teacher), or extracurricular program staff who are willing to work with you, you need to find out about your youth participants. In conversations with staff and administrators, find out the size of the group you'll work with, and some of the general characteristics of the group. For example, when working with teachers in Timber Lake, South Dakota, the teachers briefed the author on the students' ethnic background. We then selected sites for exploration with the students that represented various aspects of the students' background, from Native American ranches to German American immigrant farms. It is always desirable to fit your charrette into an existing program or set of lessons. This will help make the experience more complete for the youth participants.

Assigning Roles for the Charrette. Most charrettes will require more than one adult to run them. Therefore there are roles for each group of participants and facilitators. Think about your groups as divided into the following roles:

◆ Facilitator or Charrette Leader
◆ Kids' Assistants (assisting facilitators, i.e. planners, teachers, and other helpers)
◆ Client(s)
◆ Teachers (may play an active role or simply help maintain order)
◆ Participants (the young people)

Support Staff (food providers, bus drivers). Inform all those involved of the basic goals of the program and what their roles will be. Although this seems obvious, you need to remember that the bus driver (if you use one) will need to know the exact route and the pick-up and drop-off points as well as the schedule he or she needs to adhere to. So too, everyone else involved in the project needs specific instructions. See a sample letter of instructions appended to this chapter.

Some people will need to be kept informed at each step of the planning process. However, in most circumstances, the youth participants need an orientation just before the event itself. A more detailed discussion of this is found in Chapter 3. In addition, all participants will need a workbook, discussed later in this chapter.

Assembling Equipment. You will need to invest in supplies and equipment for the charrette.
   The basics:

◆ Base maps
◆ Pencils and colored markers
◆ Paste
◆ Foam core or construction paper
◆ Illustrations
◆ Blank sketching paper or roll of butcher's paper

Approaching Schools

If you are a planner undertaking a charrette and you wish to work with a school, you need to learn about the school. Further, you will need to develop the program with the administrators and teachers. A good place to begin is with the curriculum developer for the school or school district. Often, there is one for social sciences. In other cases, you may know a particular teacher and have an "in" through his or her classroom.

In either case, you should learn about the best age level to work with and gain an understanding of what is being taught at what grade level. Some schools already have city awareness programs or civics or local government classes. Art classes, geography, and local history may all be good entry points for a planning charrette.

These young people were so proud of their project, they decided to let their teachers share in the glory and pose with them.

Time Line for Planning

3 months in advance	Identify the project and the sponsors and/or clients Identify potential volunteers Hold first meeting to discuss the project Identify potential sources of financial support
2.5 months in advance	Determine the date, place, time, and length of the project Determine how the project will fit into the school's or organization's curriculum Obtain financial commitments from sponsors Teachers: get firm commitments from planners Planners: get firm commitments from teachers and school administrators
2 months in advance	Recruit volunteers Hold meeting for volunteers and other key people to orient them to the program Begin program planning with key people Determine whether or not all the logistics will work (i.e., Can you do a walking tour of the area? Are buses available to move students around? What number of young people do you wish to work with?) Decide on the method by which you will select your charrette topic
1.5 months in advance	Prepare first draft instructional materials for program Prepare first draft of workshop agenda Circulate all instructional materials to volunteers and teachers for review
1 month in advance	Edit and assemble instructional workbook and materials; make copies Arrange for transportation, food, and other outside logistics Brief principal or other school administrators on the project
2 weeks in advance	Hold meeting with all adult volunteers to review workbook materials and charrette outline and format
1 week in advance	Send advance materials to teachers, students, or young participants Contact the media for coverage of the live event Check with teachers, volunteers, and outside help to make certain everyone is ready
Day of the charrette	Have a checklist and use it to make certain everything you need is there; have list of phone numbers to contact people if there are problems

12:00-1:30 PM

PART 3: NEIGHBORHOOD DESIGN GAME

Neighborhood Design Game
The neighborhood design game is a tactile and interactive way of getting kids to communicate big and cool ideas for the Marina Neighborhood. The game has a number of different kinds of pieces that can be used to show how the neighborhood can be developed. It gives them a chance to discuss the types of places they want to create, and the activities they feel are important to include in the neighborhood.

Directions
The Game has two parts. The first is to record on the game board what the kids found important about the neighborhood from the neighborhood walk. The second is to identify features they would like to see in a plan of the Marina Neighborhood.

Kids Design San Pablo, General Plan Update Process

First: Mapping the Neighborhood Walk
The kids will spend the first 30 minutes of the game adding notes and pictures to the game board. After they do this, you will go through several questions with them and write down their observations on a sheet of flip chart paper. This should take about 15 minutes.

Q1: Which was the largest street? Did it seem to be the most important street, or was some other street more important?

Q2: Which was the quietest street?

Q3: Which building did you like the most? Why?

Second: Design Game
After mapping the neighborhood, you will be working with the kids to create a vision of the future for the Marina Neighborhood. The kids will use colored game pieces to show where they would like to see housing, shopping, play areas, schools or other activities they want in the neighborhood. Prior to starting this, you will ask them three questions to consider while they are designing the neighborhood.

Q1: What will be the best streets to live on?

Q2: Where do kids play or go to hang out?

Q3: Where do people in the neighborhood go shopping?

After they work on the game for about 40 minutes, help the kids talk about what the best part of their plan is. What is their biggest and coolest idea? Using the camera, take a picture of the kids standing next to their design and glue it to the game board.

page **5**

Here is a page of the workbook used in the San Diego Kids' Planning Charrette. Notice that complete instructions are given for the exercises. However, the instructions are very straightforward and easy to read.

Beyond the basics:

◆ Polaroid cameras
◆ Mylar overlays
◆ Computer and printer
◆ Graphics templates
◆ Photographs and other illustrations
◆ Blueprints
◆ GIS (Geographic Information Systems) software

Food. Having food available during the charrette helps to set an informal tone. It also serves as a reward for the youth participants for their participation. And, it can be a motivator to help get young people to participate. See the case study from Albuquerque in Chapter 1 for a discussion of how to use food and find sponsors for your program.

Tarek Monier is the Planning Director of Mason City, Iowa, but served as a Kids' Assistant at the San Diego Kids' Planning Charrette. His enthusiasm kept the kids focused and involved throughout the day.

Recording the Results. Make sure you have lined up a person to help record the results of the event. While an adult Kids' Assistant or facilitator can play this role, this is likely to be an enjoyable role for the young people. The participants will learn to summarize their work and present it to an outside audience. This topic is discussed at more length in Chapter 4. Whatever recording methods you choose, make sure they support how the results will be shared.

Legal Issues. Occasionally there may be some legal issues to deal with ahead of time. For example, are you required to get additional insurance for the use of a bus? Has someone requested that you indemnify them from legal actions during an environmental walk? Ask questions of your host institution and make sure you sort this out ahead of time so that there are not any last minute surprise costs. You want to plan carefully so the young people are safe and well cared for in case of emergencies.

PREPARING A CHARRETTE AGENDA

Don't forget to prepare a workshop agenda. A more detailed agenda will be necessary for the adults working on the charrette. Youth participants should receive a simplified version. The agenda will help you organize, stay focused and on track, and communicate the course of the project. See Appendix B at the end of this chapter as an example.

PREPARING A CHARRETTE WORKBOOK

All participants will need a workbook. The workbook contains:

◆ A brief description of the purpose and the goals of the workshop
◆ The names of the key adults the young people will be working with
◆ All the exercises with space to draw or write information
◆ Some simplified research materials such as scanned photos and maps
◆ Base maps or forms for all exercises
◆ Instructions for the exercises
◆ Instructions for the final findings of the charrette

The workbook should be simple, and it helps if it is graphically attractive and easy to read. It is absolutely vital that it contains the exercises and instructions. Having them in a workbook is convenient for the young people so they won't lose loose papers. In addition, a well-designed workbook leads the participants through the process and allows them to go back and review the building blocks of previous exercises.

To: Conference Manager, Zamorano Teachers, and Bus Drivers
From: Carolyn Torma
Subject: Charrette
Date: 29 Mar 97

Here are the logistics for the charrette event at the San Diego Children's Museum on April 7.

BUSES

Morning Pick-up: pick-up students at 9:15 a.m., April 7 at Zamorano Elementary School; bring them to San Diego Children's Museum at 200 W. Island Drive.

Afternoon Pick-up: pick-up students at 2:15 pm at San Diego Children's Museum and return them to Zamorano School; students must be back by 3:00 p.m.

Number: around 75 students and 2 teachers

The school is located at 2655 Casey Street. Casey St. is under construction and so there is a temporary bus loading zone on Tooma St. near the intersection with Casey St. where the kids will be picked up and dropped off.
School contact: Cheryl Borne p: 619-555-8007; f: 619-555-9748

At the Children's Museum, the kids will probably be left off and picked up on Union Street (west side) at the intersection of Union and Island.
Museum contact: Gwen Fowler p: 619-555-8792; f: 619-555-8796

FOOD

Lunch: We will need box lunches for students, teachers, instructors, and planners. To be safe, order for 120 people.

Morning snack: we will need a 10 a.m. morning snack (cookie and drink) for 120 people

REGISTRATION

Registration will be at the Museum on Monday morning. My assistant and I will check registrations and give out badges, etc. at the museum.

DAY'S AGENDA

See attached.

This memo was used to inform the key logistical staff of everything they needed to know to plan accordingly.

This agenda served several purposes. It alerted the logistics staff to details of the schedule. Also, it defined the sequence of the program for the adult participants.

Kids' Planning Charrette
American Planning Association
San Diego Children's Museum
200 W. Island Drive

DAY AND TIMES

Monday, April 7, 1997
8:30 a.m. - 4:30 p.m.

AGE GROUP

Elementary school, grades 5-6
Two classes

WORKSHOP OBJECTIVES

Kids
- ◆ Understanding the ingredients of a quality neighborhood
- ◆ Learning about the planning process and the role they can play through active participation
- ◆ Increasing their awareness of cities, how they function and how they are planned

Planners
- ◆ Learning how to develop a charrette program for teaching planning to kids
- ◆ Learning the principles of a kids' education program
- ◆ Having an opportunity to plan with kids

Teachers and Curriculum Professionals
- ◆ Exposing San Diego school curriculum personnel to the potential of using planning as a tool for teaching about cities and the civic process
- ◆ Providing an opportunity for planners and teachers to work together on a project

AGENDA
REGISTRATION   (8:30 a.m. - 8:45 a.m.)

Register conference attendees' kids
Planners and teachers pick up workshop materials

ORIENTATION   (8:45 a.m. - 9:30 a.m.)
Purpose of the Charrette and Day's Agenda
    10 minutes: Carolyn
Community-Based Planning Charrettes: What are They and Why Use Them?
    15 minutes: Bruce
Activity-Based Teaching
    15 minutes: Ramona

KIDS ARRIVE AND KIDS' ORIENTATION   (9:45 a.m. - 10:00 a.m.)
Food and badges for kids to pick up

KIDS WORKSHOP   (10:00 a.m. - 2:15 p.m.)
EXERCISE ONE: Cognitive Map of Their Own Neighborhood   (10:00 a.m. - 10:30 a.m.)
                Bruce, Tony, Noré
                20 minutes for work; 15 minutes for sample reporting back;
                    10 minutes for Bruce and Tony to summarize
                Planners and teachers do exercise along with kids

EXERCISE TWO: Understanding the Museum Neighborhood: Kids and Planners Walk the
                Neighborhood and Develop Conceptual Maps   (11:00 a.m. - 11:45 a.m.)
                Each team goes out with a planner and a camera and a set of things to record

EXERCISE THREE: Neighborhood Planning Features Game   (11:45 a.m. - 1:30 p.m.)
                Lunch is put out at tables for kids to eat as soon as they come back
                into the museum. Kids work with planners and teachers as technical staff
                support in developing their plans for the neighborhood

KIDS REPORT ON THEIR PLANS (1:30 p.m. - 2:00 p.m.)
                Bruce and Tony debrief

THANK YOUS, GOOD-BYES, & KIDS GET BACK ON THE BUSES
break for planners
kids leave by 2:15 p.m.

PLANNERS WORKSHOP

Summary of Day's Workshop or "What Have We Learned, Dorothy?" (2:15 p.m. - 2:45 p.m.)
    Tony

San Diego's Built Environment Education Program and the Lessons Learned   (2:45 p.m. -3:15 p.m.)
    Kay Wagner

Other Resources and Approaches to Teaching Kids (3:15 p.m. - 3:30 p.m.)
    Open Discussion led by Ramona and Kay

EXERCISE FOR PLANNER PARTICIPANTS: Designing a Charrette Around a Planning Issue in
Your Community (3:30 p.m. - 4:00 p.m.)

Debrief Exercise and Good-bye (4:00 p.m. - 4:30 p.m.)
    Bruce, Tony and Noré

FACILITATING THE CHARRETTE

CHAPTER 3

PARTICIPATION TECHNIQUES

Everyone participates—that is the golden rule of charrettes. A worthy goal, but occasionally a challenge to achieve. So, here are some useful things to keep in mind that will help achieve full participation by all the young people.

Break into Small Groups and Keep the Groups Small

Participation is very difficult in large groups and tends to allow only the most verbally self-confident to participate. Small group work allows for more opportunities to participate.

Use simple techniques to draw participants out if they get off to a slow start. For example, have each young person draw one thing on the map that they observed on the environmental walk. Have each one use a different color. Use a note board (sheet of paper taped to the wall or placed alongside the map) to record ideas that have not yet developed into full planning ideas. Show the participants how they can "park" a neat idea on the note board and come back to it at a later point in the charrette.

Breaking down a class of young participants into groups allows them to work on projects and interact with their peers in a way that fosters active participation. Eight people is an ideal size for small group work.

The All Important Kids' Assistants

Recruit enough volunteers (teachers, planners, interested adults, or older students) to have one or two at each table. Make certain they know they are performing the role of Kids' Assistant. A good orientation session for the volunteers will give them proper preparation for their roles as facilitators and not dictators. These volunteers should have a set of techniques for drawing out shy young people, keeping overly energetic ones focused, and keeping the energy level of the group high and positive.

The Role of Charrette Leader or Facilitator

One person needs to play the role of leader or facilitator. The charrette leader keeps everyone on time, explains each segment of the charrette as the group moves through it, and circulates among the groups to observe, make comments, and inject some energy. She or he must also watch the adult volunteers to make certain they don't begin to dominate the young people (a very easy mistake to make).

Charrette facilitator Bruce Race records students' discussion of his neighborhood drawing. To help with the oversight, feedback, and the final debriefing, Tony Costello was assistant facilitator. Working together they kept things moving and appropriately paced.

Pace

A good charrette is a well-paced experience that keeps everyone focused and keeps the energy level high. Like most things in facilitation, learning to pace a charrette well takes experience and

Tips on Room Set Up

Small Group Work: Set up the room so that all students and volunteers can see the leader and yet have areas where they can work together in small groups.

Staging Areas: Have areas where participants can hang or tape photographs, notes, sketch maps, and other materials on the wall or in a staging area. This allows them to keep referring to the material and integrating it when appropriate.

Allow the Young People to Adjust the Room Set-up: In the San Diego Kids' Planning Charrette, the students asked to rearrange the room at the start of the charrette. They wanted to be able to see each other easily and to get up occasionally and observe the work of another group. As a result of the rearranged room, the energy level went up and all the students felt more involved.

Break Areas: Create a place where anyone can go for a little break. Ideally, this place would have a snack, supplies, or a place for lunch.

Set-up and Clean-up: Reinforce the message of ownership of the project by having the young people participate in set-up and clean-up, when feasible.

The Kids City event at the Orlando APA National Planning Conference operated at a high energy level as young people moved from creating their buildings to siting them on a large town map. The excitement of creating and accomplishing something in one day helped to sustain the enthusiasm.

talent. Here are some basic tips that will help you.

Length of Exercises and Segments. The exercises need to be long enough to accomplish the work, but not so long that everyone loses interest. Set times for completing each segment of the charrette and give 5, 2, and 1 minute warnings for completing the tasks. Forcing the young people to conclude their work will help them focus. It will also clue them into realizing that they don't have to solve the world's problems in one afternoon.

Keeping Focused and Keeping Up the Energy Level. The charrette leader needs to circulate among the groups and drop in and listen. He or she needs to spur things along if a group has dragged down. The young people need to know that you take the work seriously and are listening and watching them. Avoid taking the project away from the participants, but do keep them moving forward.

Use Your Energy to Keep the Pace. As charrette leader, your energy level and ability to focus people quickly is very important. Start each segment with a good and energetic explanation. Don't hesitate to use humor. Keep explanations clear and simple—the young people don't need to know everything about planning; they need to know how to do the work successfully.

ORIENTATION

The youth participants need to begin with an orientation to the charrette. This orientation should not only alert the young people to the adventure ahead, but orient them to some basic planning concepts. If you are a planner, remember that both young people and their teachers need to be oriented. See sample teacher background memo appended to this chapter for an example of teacher orientation.

Orientation Exercises

A short homework assignment is a good way to start. In the appendix to this chapter is a quick city planning quiz used in the San Diego Kids' Planning Charrette. Here are some other ideas.

Orientation Exercise One: Brain Teaser

This could include:

> Questions on the history of the community in which the young people live
> Questions on the career and work of planners
> Matching planning terms to definitions (with a few funny nonsense ones thrown in)
> Matching significant dates with events in planning history
> Identification of American cities by photos or maps
> Identification of types of city maps (historic atlas, zoning, population, land use, etc.)

Orientation Exercise Two: My Family and Our Community

This could include:

> Interviews with their parents or neighbors about a current planning issue.
> Photographs that show some feature of their home community (i.e. Dad playing baseball at the baseball diamond in 1975; brother getting married in a neighborhood church, etc.).

Orientation Exercise Three: Discussion

Older youth have the ability and knowledge to discuss planning issues. The facilitator's role in this case is to help students understand how and why a local political or news issue relates to planning. A very simple technique used by an urban historian was to bring a newspaper to each class. The class began with an open-ended discussion of an issue covered in the news. In some cases it was the limits on growth the city council was attempting to place on the city, another time it was a debate over the preservation of large horse farms surrounding the city.

Orientation Exercise Four: Reading Assignments

There are many excellent books on cities that young people could read as a warm-up to a planning charrette. Among them are *Global Cities: Investigating the Ecology of Our Towns and Cities* by Philip

Guide to Developing Exercises

1. Exercises should be problem solving and require critical thinking
2. Engage as many senses and methods of communication as possible:
   writing
   observing
   group discussion
   moving around to gain a new perspective
   using space in three dimensions
3. Instructions must be clear and simple
4. Display instructions for easy reference
5. Make exercises humorous when possible
6. Use small rewards to reinforce learning
7. The exercise must be simple enough to be completed in the allotted time
8. Call upon existing knowledge
9. Each new exercise should build upon the previous one
10. Exercises should promote self-discovery
11. Leave room for creativity; use the larger environment, such as the neighborhood as the setting for excersises.
12. Make the exercises fun!

Teachers from Zamorano Elementary School helped break the ice at the start of the charrette by sitting with their students. They demonstrated their interest in the project by joining in the exercise.

Parker and *How Cities Work* by Preston Gralla. Both are suitable for a middle school-aged reader. A poster series with lesson plans that illustrate how cities change is also a good opening exercise. Renata von Tscharner and Ronald Lee Fleming are the authors of this package, *A Changing American Cityscape*. (See bibliography for all these works.)

Orientation Exercise Five: Planning History
Appended to this chapter is an exercise that introduces young people to their town. It's called "City Detective: Who Designed My Town?" This somewhat lengthy exercise would take several days to do unless all the background materials were pre-assembled. The goal is to increase young people's awareness of the design of their town and how it has changed.

Introduction to the Charrette
The second part of orientation addresses the specifics of the charrette. Young people will need to have an understanding of the overall process and the amount of time they will be devoting it. Don't underestimate your youth participants. The 7th and 8th graders in Timber Lake, South Dakota, were told they would work with the author for a week and would decide on their own final project by the end of the week. On Thursday of that week, the students confronted the author and said "that's not good enough." We then discussed and negotiated what the final project should be, how it would be carried out, and who would get to see it. The students chose to do an exhibit that addressed three thematic areas we investigated together. They chose to display the exhibit at the local historical society museum. The quality and sophistication of the exhibit was a pleasant surprise to the director of the society, who gave the students high praise. The point here is that youth participants want a clear direction to channel their ideas. And, they demanded more of the adult leader in helping them decide on their project and format. Once the Timber Lake students had that direction, they were capable of carrying out their own project with little direction from the teachers or the author.

This orientation should provide all the participants with the following:

◆ What the charrette is and why they are participating in it
◆ How long the entire charrette project will take
◆ How the schedule will be broken down (number of hours per day or week)
◆ If the young people will be doing activities outside the classroom, an explanation of what they will be doing
◆ An introduction to the volunteer planners and other adults and an explanation of what the working relationships will be
◆ An explanation of the youth participants' role

Cognitive mapping often begins with some experience of a place. Here, planners (and their children) began their environmental walk with a lunch in Boston's Chinatown in order to gain a sense of the taste, smell, and feel of a community.

◆ An idea of what the end product will be
◆ Helpful hints on attire
◆ Supplies to bring from home
    (i.e. boxes to create their buildings, photographs of the community)

CHARRETTE EXERCISE ONE

Warm-Up
Remember, all exercises should be contained in the workbook.

A warm-up exercise is the opening activity in the charrette itself. A quick and effective way to break the ice with young people is to put them to work on something immediately. An opening exercise also establishes the mood for the charrette, letting the participants know that it is active, creative, and fully participatory. This charrette guide is design oriented, therefore, it is recommended that this exercise be a warm-up in graphics skills.

Drawing is good opener, however, the exercise must be linked to the rest of the charrette. Young

In the Kids' Planning Charrette, students used Polaroid cameras to record their observations. Each team had one camera and the responsibility of photographing was shared.

people can start by drawing their neighborhood or some other aspect of their physical world. Although Roger Hart, author of *Children's Participation,* cautions that drawing can be easily dismissed by adults as unimportant, we don't agree. Planners should let the participants know that they use graphic techniques constantly in their own work. A good way to do this is in the debriefing of the warm-up exercise. You can reinforce the value of drawing by talking about how drawing is one of the graphic techniques used to explain ideas and convey information. You might show or post around the room some of the planners' sketches, drawings, maps, and graphics that illustrate how these are integral techniques and tools used by planners every day.

A drawing exercise should focus on a particular subject. It can be as open-ended as "draw your neighborhood" or more directed, such as asking students to draw:

- All the rivers, ponds, reservoirs, streams, swimming pools etc. in the community (or neighborhood if they live in a large city).
- All the kinds or transportation and routes of transportation the young people could take to go to the movie.
- All the places where their pet dogs roam, both off and on the leash.
- All the parks, open lots, and green areas in the city where the participants like to play.
- A favorite place in the community.
- All the places in the neighborhood that are associated with their family.

It's a good idea to establish the democratic nature of the charrette by having the adults do the exercise along with the young people.

Debriefing

After each major segment or activity of the charrette, it is critical that the facilitator debrief the youth participants. If the opening exercise is a drawing, then select a handful of drawings to have the students show. As facilitator, talk with the young people about what they drew and why. For example, as the students in the San Diego Kids' Planning Charrette talked about their drawings, the facilitator offered comments such as "So your neighborhood has a lot of people out on the street doing things" or "You drew this dog very large. Are there some dogs in your neighborhood that are scary?" To reinforce the value of the drawings, have the students display them and refer to them later in the charrette or have the students integrate them into their later projects.

CHARRETTE EXERCISE TWO

Selecting the Charrette Problem

If you chose to involve the young people in the selection of the problem, there is no one specific time that is "just right" to do this. You may wish to have participants do several exercises that build an understanding of planning issues before selecting the final topic. See Chapter 2 for more information on how to select a planning issue or topic. At a minimum young people need to have some familiarity with planning issues as well as with you and your team before selecting a specific topic.

Truthfully, almost all children's activities begin with the adult having an idea of where he or she wants to go with the young people. And, you (if you are a planner) have a good idea of what makes a good or weak charrette topic or (as a teacher) recognize what is possible. Therefore, you might have the youth participants undertake exercises designed to help them focus on a group of related issues (i.e. neighborhood improvements) and then have the youth participants select which particular part of the problem they wish to focus upon.

At whatever stage you articulate the problem and the goal of the charrette, it needs to be communicated to the participants. A good way to do this is this is write out the goal and post it for all to see. A large banner prepared by the participants would work nicely.

CHARRETTE EXERCISE THREE

Awareness Building

How and when you decide to define the charrette problem will determine the sequence of exercises. It is likely you will need to do some form of environmental—both natural and man-made—awareness building before you define completely the problem the charrette is designed to solve.

Following the sequence we have created here, the next step in the charrette is to move from a personal depiction of something to an activity that begins to engage the young people directly with the resources and the physical area to be explored. The participants will be taking the first step toward connecting their personal experience and perceptions to an understanding of more complex situations, environments, and relationships. There are several different activities that accomplish this. The two major things that participants should focus on in this exercise are:

◆ an understanding of the physical environment of their problem area and
◆ an understanding of the information needed to record and analyze the problem.

There are several pre-packaged programs for environmental awareness walks and surveys. One, created by the Center for Understanding the Built Environment, is *Walk Around the Block*. This program is geared to an elementary school age level. Two publications demonstrate some simple and effective survey projects: *The Kid's Guide to Service Projects* and *The Kid's Guide to Social Action*. These projects are for middle school-aged youth. *Community as a Learning Resource* by Ramona Mullahey is a great source of exercises that can be adapted to a planning charrette. (See the bibliography.)

A Survey

Young people can conduct a survey by recording information systematically. This approach works especially well with charrettes focused on historic preservation or a specific group of people. One innovative program is *Youth Mapping*. In this program, young people map indicators (factual information about the neighborhood or community, such as the number of libraries or the rate of teenage pregnancy). They look at all types of resources and even delve more deeply into the information by asking questions such as, "How many hours is the public library open when school is not in session?" The young people then map this information to create a composite picture of where the community stands today and how it might improve tomorrow. For example, they might show that a youth map of one neighborhood reveals that there are 65 pupils per computer in the schools, while a nearby community has a ratio of 10 pupils to one computer.

Physical Environment Survey. Using cameras, maps, and survey forms, young people can record individual buildings or entire streetscapes. In environmental charrettes, students might conduct inventories of birds and animals around the school yard. You will need to provide guidance on what to record and how. In the case of a bird inventory, for example, young people need a bird spotters' guide. It is important to tailor the surveys and survey forms to the age group of the surveyors. The survey cannot be overly complex, but it must be meaningful.

In the San Diego Kids' Planning Charrette, the entire event was only a few hours. The students were broken into teams with adult facilitators. Every student and adult was given a walking tour map of the neighborhood, illustrated on the following page. Five places on the walk were marked as stopping points. At each one, students were asked to make a record of what they observed on their map and with the Polaroid camera. Each team had one camera and students took turns photographing.

In Timber Lake, students walked through their small town with maps and, as in the example above, stopped at pre-designated spots. At each spot they had to look for a specific feature, such as a building material, the width of the street, or the type of housing; record what they saw; and discuss what they now knew about its meaning. For example, they observed that a storefront was made of metal and had been manufactured in Ohio and therefore had been shipped to the town by rail.

Interviewing People Survey. A survey can also be made of the people who are affected by the study topic or problem. For example, if your topic is *improving the neighborhood for the elderly*, then elderly people would be surveyed to find out what they see as problems. The survey could also

NEIGHBORHOOD WALK

STOP 1: MARKET STREET
STOP 2: HORTON PLAZA
STOP 3: THIRD AVENUE
STOP 4: CHILDREN'S PARK
STOP 5: HARBOR DRIVE

record the elderly population, the special residences for the elderly, and social institutions and businesses that serve the elderly. Again, surveys should be specific and well focused.

In Timber Lake, students were assigned to interview their parents. The topics was *historic preservation and community history*. Each student was asked: (1) how long the family had lived in the community; (2) where had the family lived prior to Timber Lake; (3) what was their ethnic or cultural background; (4) to create a list of all the houses or dwelling places their family had lived in the town. The next day many students arrived with not only their surveys, but photographs of their families that were posted on the board with their surveys.

Conducting Research. Youth participants can also learn to collect the data that will help them define and understand their charrette problem. As mentioned before, you can choose to do this research work yourself or have students undertake it as part of the charrette. Also, as mentioned previously, they would gather population data, maps, sites plans, photographs and other graphic information, reports, and other planning materials. A word of caution. Since much of this material will be spread out over many offices and agencies, this can be a very time consuming and even frustrating step in the process. Therefore, pre-assembling information may be the wisest approach. See also Chapter 2 for more information on conducting research.

Primary resources (maps, drawings, demographic information, etc.) may need some interpretation. Therefore, exercises or lessons on reading data and primary resource information may be necessary. Make the research information visible throughout the charrette. In that way, the participants can refer to it and be reminded that they are building upon their own research as well as their ideas and observations.

CHARRETTE EXERCISE FOUR
Mapping
No better description exists for explaining the primacy of maps to planning than Roger Hart's. Mapping should be an essential part of any planning charrette; mapping helps make issues visible.

Using Published Mapping Exercises. You may chose to focus your charrette almost exclusively on mapping. If so, there are two publications that you can use. Barbara Taylor's *Maps and Mapping* is an excellent introduction to the subject of cartography and has some good short exercises. The book focuses on the purposes and techniques of cartography; however, you will need to add the planning dimension. Another publication that offers more games and exercises is *How to Draw Maps and Charts* by Pam Beasant and Alastair Smith. This publication explores several varieties of graphic information that are displayed spatially. (See bibliography.)

Creating a Map. In the exercises discussed previously, the facilitator provided the young people with the map that ordered their exercise experience. In this next phase of the charrette you want the participants to generate their own map. This doesn't mean that the starting point is a blank sheet of paper; indeed, providing a consistent set of *base* maps for the participants to work with will likely help them orient quickly and work consistently to define and refine the problem and the solution.

As an example, in the San Diego Kids' Planning Charrette, once the students returned from the environmental awareness walk, they sat down with large base maps of the neighborhood that showed streets, rail lines, the footprint of buildings, and the park. The kids took turns recording their observations and, through discussion, began to make some sense of what they observed. Planners are skilled at developing base maps.

Mapping may make clear the ways in which various issues are related and need to be acted on together because of their systemic nature.
Roger Hart

Displaying Collected Data—Overlay Maps. Other maps can include the visual display of survey data—location of parks, pathways, location of environmental resources, such as wetlands, etc. Depending on the project, students can develop overlays on one large base map or work in groups and find group solutions to problems through their own project map. The exercise sheets in the workbook provided to the youth participants should guide the recording of information on the base map. The base map may be large enough that it needs to be separate from the workbook.

The point of the mapping exercise is to display the information they have gathered and to begin to order and make sense of that information in a visual medium. A map by itself may not suffice. The participants may wish to record some ideas on flip chart paper or the chalk board. In Timber Lake, the "map" the students created was a measured drawing of a historic house. Teams of students assembled, on one large site plan or map, all the individual measurements they had done of the yard and garden, the footprint of the house, the floor plan of the interior, and the placement of the garage, walkways, and clothesline.

Collage. Another approach to mapping is collage, a mixture of elements such as photographs, drawings, notations, time lines, and a base map. The student workshops based on the Cooper Hewitt Museum's *A City of Neighborhoods* education program have young people create a neighborhood collage. The goal of this program is to develop a historical awareness of the young peoples' own neighborhood. Secondarily, it helps them recognize and learn to address current problems within the neighborhood. The youth participants record and then recreate a streetscape in their neighborhood using their own photographs, drawings, maps, and other printed materials, which are organized into a large collage. Roger Hart offers this observation:

"In collages, images are often chosen by intuition or pleasure with colour and forms. Collage making seems to increase the visualizing capabilities. Also, the possibility of contrasts in scale—for example, a sheep as large as a public housing tower—can have symbolic and metaphoric potential that children often do not feel free to express in drawing. A mixture of expressive forms—photos, colours, words, and drawings—is almost always richer in content than only one means of expression. . . . Thus, the process of choosing images, cutting, pasting, and positioning can contribute to the goals of collaborative work."

Gaming. Yet a fourth approach is to use a game with a game board and pieces. The game board is a template or a simple map of the area being addressed in the charrette. In San Diego at the Kids' Planning Charrette the game consisted of:

◆ Game board: a simplified base map of the neighborhood showing streets, footprints of the buildings, rail lines, and a park. This was printed on an 18" x 36" sheet. One sheet for each team.

The first map series the students worked on for the San Diego charrette were an energetic amalgam of every group member's ideas.

At the Boston Children's Museum, planners learned to develop a children's exhibit about the Chinatown neighborhood. The exercise incorporated contemporary planning issues into an exhibit about the present-day and historic ethnic neighborhood.

◆ Game pieces: foam core pieces with colored paper glued on the top. Each piece was labeled with building or land-use types, such as: house, museum, shopping center, garage, apartment building, homeless shelter, bus station, etc.
◆ Colored pens: used to make notations on the map—including greenways, major and minor roads, direction of traffic—and to add features that were not accounted for in the game pieces.
◆ Photographs: Polaroid photographs that helped illustrate points were also attached to the game board. The photographs had been taken during the environmental walk.

The plan created by the youth participants was the completed game board with the pieces glued to the board and the notations written on the map/board that explained their ideas for the neighborhood.

Gaming has some great advantages. The game pieces are dimensional and so allow users to see and think in three-dimensional space. Buildings, land uses, and base maps can be combined in a quick and easy manner by the participants. Like collage, it overcomes reservations young people may have about their drawing skills. Also, the game allows for several layers of complexity at once. Further, it appears more accessible, familiar, and perhaps fun to young people than starting with a flat map.

As these examples illustrate, mapping should not be a solitary activity, it should be collaborative. The collaboration allows young people to talk, discuss, make points, disagree, negotiate, and refine their map. For adults, at this stage in the charrette it sometimes is an overwhelming temptation to tell the young people what they have seen. It is better to wait for the observation to emerge. When a participant makes an observation or assertion, your role is to raise some questions for the group to consider.

Ideally, the young people will have an opportunity to create a "first draft" of their final map. This first draft will often be a very high-energy image, filled with bold and even chaotic-seeming lines and suggestions. Allowing the opportunity for the participants to start over and refine their work will allow them to "rewrite," rethink, and develop more order to ideas, observations, and eventual proposed solutions.

CHARRETTE EXERCISE FIVE
The Final Project

The final project is really storytelling. The story the young people will be telling is what their experience has been, what new things they have learned, and where they would like things to go from here. Each person or group will develop its own narrative based on how they have put those three critical pieces together.

For charrettes of relatively short duration, such as the San Diego Kids' Planning Charrette, the

final project was the verbal report on the plans and the debriefing led by the charrette leader. However, when possible you will want to give the young people more time to let their ideas mature and to develop more complex stories for their plans.

In Chapters 4 and 5, the final project is discussed in more detail. Let's proceed here to the debriefing portion of the charrette.

DEBRIEFING

There is an art to debriefing. Practice is the best way to build your skills as a facilitator and debriefer. It can also be helpful to work with a partner—one person observing and interacting with the participants and one recording the observations for the final summation.

Bruce Race, the charrette leader, guided students through their presentations and debriefing, while assistant Tony Costello graphed the ideas and issues that the students addressed in their plan. The graphic was used in the final summation of the charrette.

Three Big and Cool Ideas

We recommend using the technique of *three big and cool ideas* as a way of focusing the youth participants' work. It is all too easy to lose ideas in planning under the barrage of "everything is connected to everything." Therefore, remember that the goal of debriefing is clarity and simplicity that reinforces understanding. As part of the instruction sheets that each youth participant receives in his or her workbook is the outline for writing down their three big and cool ideas. Their projects may be complex, but if they are forced to report on only three things, this will help them set priorities for their observations and learn to summarize for other people.

Some steps for the facilitator/kids' assistant to follow in the debriefing process:

◆ Everyone or every group reports on their work; it must be inclusive.
◆ Allow the young people to select their own spokesperson for the group.
◆ Have each group focus on its three big and cool ideas.
◆ Have the students show how these are illustrated in their project.
◆ The leader can draw out the participants with questions and observations.

Your assistant will record on a flip chart or on the board. The observations should be ordered in some way. One method of doing this is to create a grid, using topic headings is another. A grid allows the facilitator to make connections between ideas by displaying them graphically. As the assistant listens to the responses, he or she can begin to sort them into categories. So, for example, in the San Diego Kids' Planning Charrette, a common issue for the participants was how to redirect traffic to make some streets feel safer and quieter (*Traffic Circulation* was the column heading). Design solutions included allowing faster-moving traffic only on streets at the edges of the neighborhood and putting low speed limits on other streets (i.e. various solutions were listed in rows by work group). As several groups addressed the traffic issue in their plans, the assistant facilitator characterized this as "traffic and circulation." He then placed a dot in the column and row that related to the topic. The illustration on the following page is more detailed and uses short phrases to capture the ideas. Counting the dots or linking up the ideas helps the participants see where consensus may be forming around issues.

Debriefing of *Kids' Planning Charrette*				
Group	**Traffic and Circulation**	**Play Areas**	**Shopping**	**Housing**
One: Sarah's Group	busy street—Meridian Blvd. only; other streets local	add 2 play lots for young kids	make Horton Plaza for kids only most of the day	build more tall apartment buildings
Two: Seth's Group	kid mobiles to move kids around		add stores along Spruce Street	put housing on top of garages
Three: Arnie's Group	put more stop signs on Elm St. to let kids cross over to school safely	make greenway that connects to school	put McDonald's near school	build houses in empty lots
Four: Susan's Group	close Elm St. to cars	add more play area to Kids Park; let kids get in the water		add homeless shelter along Spruce St.

Lawrence Chang, an architect and planner, joined the Children's Museum staff in debriefing the exhibit plans created by APA planners. He brought a community perspective and insider's insight into the debriefing process that made the final exercise more meaningful for the participants.

Appendix A illustrates the background memo that was sent to teachers to prepare them for the charrette.

American Planning Association
KIDS' PLANNING CHARRETTE
San Diego Children's Museum
April 7, 1997

BACKGROUND FOR TEACHERS

You and your class will be joining city planners for a day of exercises focused on neighborhoods. We'll be asking the students three questions: What is a neighborhood? How do we analyze a neighborhood? How do we plan for a neighborhood?

The event is being held in conjunction with the American Planning Association's annual conference. The conference is the professional conference for America's city planners, some of whom are interested in involving their communities in planning through children's education. Twenty-five planners and a few of their children will be participating with you in the charrette.

What is a Charrette?

A charrette is a problem solving activity. A group of people, most often a combination of professionals and residents of a community spend a day looking at specific problems in a distinct area of the community. Throughout the day, they engage in exercises that help them define the problem and create suggested solutions to the problem.

Travel and Other Logistics

Time: APA will provide transportation by bus to and from the museum. Students will be picked up at 9:15 a.m. at the temporary bus loading zone on Tooma Street. Students will return to the school between 2:45 and 3:00 p.m.

Lunch: We will provide a box lunch for students and teachers, as well as a morning refreshment break.

Dress

Teachers and students should dress comfortably. You will be spending some time outside walking in the neighborhood, as well as working inside at tables or on the floor of the museum.

What is Planning?

Planning is the application of foresight to action.

City and regional planning is a profession designed to develop and improve cities. The goal is to create attractive, safe, healthful, and efficient environments for all people both in the present and in the future. Planning is city building, and takes its place alongside the other city building professions, such as architecture and engineering.

Planners are not solitary designers, rather they plan within a collaborative process. Through this process they help community members to define a vision for the community. They work with local residents, politicians, business people, and special groups.

Do the Students and I Need to Prepare?
If you wish, you may distribute the enclosed one-page quiz to your students to get them thinking about cities and planning. We recommend that you explain to students where they are going and something of what they will be doing for the day—learning to help plan a neighborhood.

Questions?
Call Carolyn Torma, at 312-431-9100. Ms. Torma and other APA staff and faculty will be with you throughout the charrette at the San Diego Children's Museum.

Carolyn Torma
Education Manager
American Planning Association
122 S. Michigan Ave., Ste. 1600
Chicago, IL 60603

This is the brain-teaser, warm-up exercise used for the San Diego Kids' Planning Charrette. It can be easily adapted to your community.

American Planning Association
Kids' Planning Charrette
Brain Teaser

Select the answer or answers:

1. The actor Kevin Bacon, who starred in the movie *Sleepers*, has a famous father who is a
    a. television actor
    b. city planner
    c. doctor
    d. architect

2. The word "city" comes from the Latin word for
    a. citrus fruit
    b. big place
    c. sky
    d. citizen

3. The oldest city (recorded on a plan or map) in the United States is
    a. New York, New York
    b. Sante Fe, New Mexico
    c. St. Augustine, Florida
    d. Seattle, Washington

4. The city of San Diego developed from a mission started by the
    a. Spanish
    b. Norwegians
    c. English
    d. French

5. 100 years ago maps were made with lengths of chain, large sheets of paper or leather, and transepts (instruments that looked like telescopes). Today, maps are made with which of the following
    a. movie cameras mounted on trucks
    b. cameras mounted on airplanes
    c. computerized cameras mounted on satellites
    d. people standing on tall buildings drawing what they see on paper

6. A city planner must have which of the following skills and knowledge
- a. ability to work well with groups of people
- b. understanding of economics and math
- c. ability to use computers
- d. ability to imagine the future

Answers:

1. b. Edmund H. Bacon was the City Planning Director for Philadelphia and is the author of the book *Design of Cities*.

2. d. The words "city" and "citizen" are both related to the word "civilization." Civilization means a society or group of people which has developed to the point of creating cities. Usually the society has developed agriculture and trading to support the city.

3. c. St. Augustine, Florida, was founded in 1564 by Spanish explorers and is considered the first American city, because it was documented with a city map or plan. Native Americans had developed some cities before the arrival of European explorers. Cahokia, Illinois, along the Mississippi River is an example. However, these cities were not recorded and mapped until many years after their founding.

4. a. The Spanish sailed the Pacific Ocean and founded the mission at San Diego in 1769.

5. b. and c. Most contemporary city maps are based on photographs taken from planes. Larger maps are made from photographs taken by satellite cameras.

6. a. - d. City planners need all these skills. Most city planners have a college education and a master's degree in city and regional planning.

Are you interested in learning more about planners? You may write the American Planning Association for a *career kit* or visit our web site at www.planning.org for more information. Write or call:

Career Information
American Planning Association
122 S. Michigan Avenue, Suite 1600
Chicago, IL 60603
312-431-9100

APPENDIX C

Appendix C is an exercise that can be used as a warm-up to familiarize young people with how cities were planned. It is a lengthy exercise and may take several class sessions to complete.

CITY DETECTIVE

Who Designed My Town?

A Lesson in Plats, Maps and Plans

Your case: Your town is a community with a past. Your town has a distinctive shape, design and layout. How has it changed? Are there any clues as to what the town was like for the first citizens of your community? Can you discover the original designer of your town? How about the original design?

Your assignment: as a detective, you must:
◆ search for clues
◆ follow those clues to the information source
◆ interpret the evidence

Getting started: you will uncover answers to the following:
What evidence is there of your town's original design?

When was it designed?

What did it look like?

Who designed it?

Your clues and where you need to go:
1. Legally, a plat of the town had to be drawn and then filed as an official record. What is a plat? Where will you find it recorded?

2. Sometimes the original plat does not exist? What other evidence is there of the early design of your town?

3. Are there any early photographs or illustrations showing your town? Where will you find them?

4. Has anyone written a history of your town? What can you find out about the design of your town from this history?

5. Most changes to the town's design (plat) are recorded and new maps made to show those changes. Who makes these changes and maintains these maps? Who draws the new city map?

Interpreting the evidence: Follow your clues to the source of information on each of the questions listed above. Once you have identified the evidence, assemble the information you have uncovered. Compare the original plat or plans to a current map of the city. Come back to class prepared to interpret it by answering the following questions.

1. Who drew the earliest plan or plat for your town?
◆ What was his/her name?
◆ Did she/he have a title?
◆ Does it appear on the plat?

2. When was your town's first plat or plan drawn?

3. When was your town founded?

4. Who founded your town?
◆ a land investment company
◆ a religious group
◆ a manufacturing company
◆ a mining company
◆ a railroad company
◆ a European government
◆ a Native American group
◆ the U.S. government
◆ other

5. Compare the earliest and current maps and plats; how has your town changed?

6. Have some of the original features changed? Why?

7. What is a plat?

8. What is a plan?

9. What is a map?

Teacher's Instructions

Purpose: The purpose of this exercise is to introduce students to some of the tools of city design, such as maps, plans, and plats.

Objectives: Students will also learn about the earliest town designs through the use of primary historical materials, such as plats. Students will also learn some of the vocabulary of planning, such as plats, plans, bird's-eye views, and maps. In addition, they will learn to compare the representations of the historic town with the present design and draw conclusions about change over time.

Relevant classes: Classes for which this exercise is suitable: social studies, civics, history, geography, and art. Age level: 10-14

The information needed and where to find it: The students will need to visit the following places:

original plat: the county courthouse–register of deeds' office
early plans, maps, and photographs: the historical society or historic preservation commission
contemporary maps: the town planning office–town plan and map file
town history and other historic materials: town library–historical collection

You may assign students the task of gathering the information. In this case, begin by giving the students the work sheet. Next, provide students some background information on how to follow the clues. Divide the students into teams and assign each team one clue. As the students uncover the information, ask them to make copies of the plans, plats, and earliest depictions (i.e. bird's-eye view maps) of the town.

If you do not want the students to leave the classroom, you may gather copies of this information before hand. Place all the copies of plats, maps, photographs, and other materials in folders. Mark each folder with the type of information and name of the place you found the information. Divide the students into groups and assign them one question from "interpreting the evidence." Have the student groups review each folder. In a class discussion, piece together the answers to the "interpreting the evidence" section.

To enrich this exercise
Invite the any of the following to join the class:
planner from the town planning department

historical society member
historic preservation commission member
staff member from the *register of deeds* office

These resource people can participate in the search, explain the function of their office or program, give insight into the development of the town, and comment on the students' findings. They can also help make comparisons between the historic and present-day town. They may also discuss future changes and their effects.

Also, if you wish to extend the lesson, consider exploring with your students the following questions:

1. What is the original and oldest part of town?

2. How was the land divided originally?
◆ Are commercial and residential lots different in shape and size?
◆ Where are the commercial lots concentrated?
◆ Where are residential lots located?
◆ Does the plan take into account natural features?
◆ Are there any parks or open spaces?
◆ Is space reserved for special uses, i.e. churches, schools, courthouse?

3. Compare today's plan to the original plan or plat. Ask the questions:
◆ How have the uses of the land in the town changed?
◆ Where is the commercial activity?
◆ Where are the residential areas?
◆ What do open spaces look like?
◆ Does the town appear to be oriented to any feature, i.e. river, freeway, lake?
◆ How has new technology had an impact?
◆ Are there any issues occurring today that may change the design of the town in the future?

For information on other teaching products on urban and regional planning:
Planners Book Service
American Planning Association
122 S. Michigan Avenue, Suite 1600
Chicago, IL 60603
312-431-9100

The planning process youth go through should anticipate how they will ultimately express their issues. Here CES students in San Francisco's Chinatown present their management plan for the process.

RECORDING THE RESULTS

One of the primary responsibilities of a facilitator is to record the results of a charrette. Recording the results of workshops and charrettes is critical to the credibility of a process in the eyes of young participants. Proper recording expands young participants' planning vocabulary and increases their understanding of issues. In turn, this allows young people to be more effective spokespersons and advocates for important issues affecting them.

WHAT TO RECORD

As a facilitator, you will ask young people to visualize their ideas, express their ideas and feelings verbally, and help them define the types of actions they or the community should take. In the previous chapter, the description of the debriefing segment of the charrette gives you specific tips on how to draw out the ideas of the young people in the debriefing. This chapter focuses more on the content of what is be debriefed and how to document the charrette. It might be helpful to think of *recording the results* as the creation of a plan.

The charrette should be as self-documenting as possible. The results of the exercises and the sharing of ideas should become part of the presentations made by participants at the end of the charrette. Methods for recording could include mapping, drawing, model building, and written summaries of verbal presentations.

Young participants should understand how important it is to communicate their views from the beginning of the process. Younger children will need exercises that are completely self-documenting and easy to publish. Older kids can participate in further definition through the creation of a communications and media plan for the charrette's results.

Youths' View of the Issues

Ideas generated by a youth charrette or workshop can enlighten the entire community, therefore, developing effective means of communicating the results to the community is important. As we've observed before, the views of youth are often overlooked by planners and adults engaged in planning. Most critically, young peoples' views reflect the needs and perspectives of families. Young participants provide insights into how communities and cultures interact, into the "street level" physical and social issues, and how national social and economic issues affect their community.

These are just a few of the ways young people can make contributions to the community's understanding of issues.

Youth and Families. Young people have distinct types of daily activities that form patterns over time. These patterns reflect their families' routines. One way to make the connection between public issues, planning, and young peoples' daily lives is to have them examine those activities. Ask participants to consider how the community supports families or creates obstacles to the family's routine, such as grocery shopping, visiting relatives, going to the doctor, etc. Have the young people consider this question: Is the community, neighborhood, or housing project a "family friendly" place?

Community and Social Relationships. Young people have a distinct view of the levels of social interaction in a community. As a result, they tend to define communities differently than do adults. Often their "innocent" views make us aware of things we adults take for granted. As you debrief the participants and help them record the results of their charrette, consider how they are expressing the community's social and cultural interactions. A simple example: Where do young people play? Is it always in the planned parks, playing fields, and tot lots? Or do young people use the entire community as a giant playing field with special areas for special activities?

When youth consider planning issues within their political context, their understanding can create a strong advocacy position. This CES student drew symptom and cause diagrams of the top three health issues facing her community.

National Issues and Local Issues. Many of the issues that youth perceive at a local level have national or regional significance. Homelessness, crime, race relations, and environmental issues often come up during planning workshops with youth. No matter how carefully you may have defined your charrette problem, there will often be larger and more complex issues such as these that will be introduced by the participants. As the facilitator you should allow these issues to emerge and be prepared to think about how they can be addressed at a local level. As we've said before, a charrette is not going to solve grave social issues, but it is an excellent opportunity to explore some of them and to listen to what young people propose as solutions.

The charrette process is a learning experience not only for the participants, but for you as well. To provide an effective lesson, you need to help the young people capture their views. Young people need to see how their own story is recorded.

How Youth Define Change

The young person's perspective of the future can be fanciful, financially or politically infeasible, or technically challenged. However, at the core of young participants' analysis and ideas is often an issue or idea that reflects their concerns and vision about the community in which they live.

In a charrette process with very young participants (K-5), the participants are given an assignment. Older kids, on the other hand, can help define the issues they want to explore. In determining the topic for the charrette, young people most often look for things they want to change. As a facilitator, your job is to provide them with the tools to express themselves, to define what they value, and to communicate their ideas on what should be changed, and how it should be changed. A facilitator provides participants with the techniques to settle on priorities for addressing issues and for finding solutions.

Defining Change. Facilitators use prompter questions (see definition in the Foreword) to get young people to focus their analysis and clarify their ideas. This "Socratic method" is preferable to telling participants what to do, but a facilitator needs to create a framework within which young participants and their assistants work. An example of a prompter question that helps young people use comparisons as way of clarifying their ideas is: "What's different about your view of the future than what exists now?" The facilitator has to capture the participants' view of what change looks like in their words. Other means of capturing ideas, as discussed before, include maps, drawings, or sketches.

How to Change. Young people often have ideas with very direct solutions. For example, an adult's approach to the problem of dirty streets might be to increase the city maintenance budget for street cleaning. Young people, on the other hand, might say we need to educate kids about why littering is a bad idea. In this case the kids are probably closer to defining the problem and to addressing its

Having a predetermined presentation format for young planners can help keep them focused on the message.

solution. At the very least, they have added a dimension to the discussion of the overall solution.

Priorities. In a world of possibilities, youth need to learn how to clearly express their priorities. Capturing the "first three things to do" or what "three things are most important about the future" (or what we called *three big and cool ideas* in Chapter 3) is a way to get participants to select and define more clearly their priorities. As young citizen advocates, reaching consensus on priorities and articulating them is at the core of shaping policy to improve community life.

Action and Advocacy Plans

Once the charrette has been recorded, the next step for the youth participants is advocacy. How can recording the results help them become effective advocates? The process of recording should include discussion of who makes decisions and how they are made relative to their charrette issue. If need be, refer to the Foreword to review who the people and groups are that make decisions in the planning process. The group of decision makers may be bigger than this "official" list and can obviously include people such businessmen or women. Clarifying this allows them to shape their message and move along to the next step of preparing a communications and media plan.

Who Makes Decisions and How. Charrettes, as a civics lesson, allow young people to make the connection between what they want done and how to make it happen. As the young people establish priorities, discuss with them who has the power to make decisions and how they make them. Ask the participants, "Of the things you have done in today's workshop, what do you think will help someone make a decision?" This may be an area in which young people are the least knowledgeable. Planners and teachers can provide some very useful information on whose domain problems fall under and who has resources for addressing these problems. At this point in the process youth start to realize they are "a force."

Defining the Message. For young participants, learning how to agree on their priorities through an interactive charrette is a significant social and intellectual breakthrough or stage of development. They get to see how this experience allows them to refine their message for policymakers or the media. By the end of the charrette they can be asked, "List your top three priorities and how you would communicate these to others," and respond confidently.

The Communications Plan. For older youth, developing a communications plan is a key element in the charrette. One team can take as their assignment the preparation of a communication plan that is reported to the entire group during the reporting segment of the charrette. The communication plan is developed first for the client(s), and secondly for the media. It should include the issues identified in the charrette, the proposed solutions, and the priorities for their ideas and proposed solutions. In addition, it should suggest how to use the media.

HOW TO RECORD THE RESULTS

As a facilitator of a youth charrette, how can you help participants record and communicate the results? As discussed in Chapter 3, having a clear set of learning and activity objectives is important prior to a charrette. This will help you identify the best methods for participants to use for recording and communicating the results.

In developing the design of the charrette, it is important to consider the audiences for the charrette results. As mentioned previously, this could include the charrette group itself, the sponsoring organization or client, the media, and other post-charrette presentation audiences.

Recording for the Charrette Group

A top-notch charrette will incorporate the opportunity for young people to record the activities and the results themselves. This makes consensus building easier and makes the process "transparent." Transparency means everything has been discussed and shared openly. A transparent process makes successful charrettes a credible tool for education, consensus building, and advocacy. Any number of methods and tools can be used to allow the charrette to be interactive and the process transparent.

Here are three example methods that demand the facilitator to be an "active listener."

Round Table Listing. As youth participants work in planning teams or small groups, they share their views on a subject. For example, the group may be sharing what they feel are the three most exciting places for kids in their community. As each participant tells the group his or her favorite places, another member of the group writes it down on a flip chart. Every time there is agreement about a place a check mark is put next to it. After each person has spoken, the group can see that the most popular places have the most check marks. At that point the group can discuss the top three places and see if everyone agrees that they should be the group's top picks.

Common Feature Maps. In Chapter 3, we discussed mapping as a recording method. We cannot emphasize strongly enough how effective maps are for allowing kids to express their understanding about their community. As the charrette progresses, they will illustrate their conception of the future. As the youth participants present their maps to the large group, the facilitator will begin to see the common features identified by participants. The facilitator can summarize these features on a blank map and lead a discussion to form consensus on the key features. This allows the participants to see where there is agreement, both in terms of locations of activities and elements, and in terms of ideas about the community.

These students on an AIA environmental walk are mapping their observations. Next, they combined their observations to create a map that identified existing site features they considered important.

Creating Categories. Some times as a facilitator, it is better to keep your questions general. This allows you to see what categories of answers or issues participants provide. Here's an example of how you might refine the ideas through increasingly specific observations or questions. As the charrette discussion begins, the charrette participants planning a park have "a hundred ideas." Using the graph method described in Chapter 3, you notice early on that the ideas fall into four categories and so you create a graph with these headings: recreation, park design, kids participation in park management, and landscaping. As the discussion continues, you also begin to notice that the participants are more interested in organized recreation than in planting trees. At that point, you may create a more detailed list under recreation. Using further questions, you challenge them to consider the specific types of organized recreation, as well as who makes the decision about these types. Finally, you would probe the participants for ideas on how to influence the decision.

Recording for the Sponsor

The charrette sponsor may be a school, community organization, or government agency. Remember, the client or sponsor is not just the young peoples' client, the client or sponsor is yours as well. The sponsor's interests in the results of a youth charrette reflect the mission of the sponsor or client group. In creating the communication plan, young people should be aware that their ideas will need to meet the expectations of the sponsor or client. Here are some tips to keep in mind.

Schools. School administrators want to see educational results. This could include demonstrating how participants improved their graphic, writing, verbal communication, and analytical skills. Therefore, you and your charrette participants will need to create a product that displays these skills. You can consider doing a show, an installation of a model or exhibit, or a special presentation by the students. In developing the design of your charrette, consider how the charrette will provide the "product" for these events.

Community-based Organizations. Many community-based organizations' missions focus on what makes the community better for kids and families. The results of the charrettes can influence the organizations' advocacy agenda. One example comes from the St. Johns Education Center. A youth charrette done for this sponsor focused on San Francisco's Mission District and resulted in the creation of a safe streets program and focused efforts to create a new park. As the charrette leader and facilitator, you need to consider whether the charrette will be used to steer an organization's agenda or further their youth advocacy efforts. Consider whether the results of the charrette can be incorporated into grant proposals.

In Albuquerque, interviewing the participants in the charrette was part of the recording of the project. This information was used as part of the final presentation of the project plan.

Government Agencies or Communities. Many planning efforts are missing a youth perspective on the community. Consider how the charrette and its proposals can be integrated into local planning efforts. Develop some formats for communicating the young peoples' work to policymakers and others. With the participants, develop some ideas on which elements of the charrette will help communicate their ideas best.

The impact of the San Diego Kids Planning Charrette was extended through the coverage provided by the local newspaper.

Recording for the Media

Youth planning projects are often media magnets. The planner or teacher who seeks publicity for the project can most often simply alert the press to the charrette program and a reporter and camera person will show up at an appointed time. It is a good idea to let the participants think about how to package their message as part of a media plan for the charrette.

When the Media Show Up. If you contact both the print and TV media, you must understand that the cameras and notebooks have a presence. Arrange for a visit at a time that illustrates the charrette process well. Press reporters, and especially TV crews, are not going to spend a whole day at the charrette. Recommend they come towards the end of the event to see how kids are working and listen to their presentations. The young people will do the rest. You can prepare a press kit that includes:

◆ workshop materials
◆ an explanation of the sponsor
◆ charrette objectives and agenda
◆ list or description of participants.

Final Charrette Presentation

The presentation of the final product or plan is often the culmination of the charrette. When the students have finished the exercises outlined in Chapter 3, they will have engaged the issue directly themselves. To complete the process, the participants should present their issues, ideas, and recommendations. It is best if the facilitator provides a common format for the presentations. This will help the participants see where they have consensus and sharpen how they present their collective recommendation at future presentations.

The participants may have to redo their graphics into a more polished format, prepare a written report that summarizes the project and its findings, and develop a script for an oral presentation. In addition, the participants will need to decide who will speak for them and how they want the presentation to be shaped. As facilitator, you will need to ascertain how much time the sponsor or client is willing to devote to this debriefing and what format he or she needs.

The following questions can be used to help organize presentations:

1. What are your top three favorite things/places in the area?

2. What are the top three issues that need to be addressed?

3. What are the three most important features or ideas in your plan?

(If there is time, and the kids are mature enough, items 4 and 5 could be added to the agenda.)

4. What are the three most important actions that need to take place to realize your plan?

5. What are the three most important messages that should be communicated about the planning issues and solutions?

These young people used "three big and cool ideas" to organize their presentation on a kids' block for San Francisco.

CHAPTER 5

These Albuquerque youth found communicating with each other to be an important part of the planning experience.

USING THE RESULTS

Empowerment and Advocacy

In Chapter 4 we discussed recording the results of a charrette, and now we turn to post-charrette advocacy activities. As suggested throughout this guide, charrettes can be a prelude to action. For educators and planners, the charrette provides guidance on how to be advocates for funding and planning for young peoples' concerns. And, you can help youth to get their ideas in motion.

NEW ISSUES: THE PERSPECTIVE OF YOUTH

As a result of the charrette, the youth have developed many new ideas. What do you do about it? In many cases youth charrette participants are the first to explore a planning issue. The kids may be anxious to share their observations and share their vision with adults. This is a sign of a successful charrette.

Young Peoples' Perspective of the Future

It is not always what youth say, but how they view the world and its future that can provide the most insight. Young peoples' perspective and social vantage point allows them to think freely about the future and ask the questions adults sometimes overlook. Their perspective on urban issues is quite different. "Is the street safe for kids? Do I have a safe and fun place to go? Who can I trust? Where can I ride my bike?" As adults we say that the most livable towns and cities are wonderful places for children; a youth charrette can remind us of how well or how poorly our communities are meeting this expectation. If the young peoples' view is informed and communicated well, a presentation event can be awesome and inspiring for adults.

A Young Person's Perspective. What is important to kids should be important to society. Never underestimate a young person's perspective on an issue. They use cities differently. They explore the underbelly of informal open space systems, walk and ride bikes, and "hang out" with a kids' pace and curiosity. Therefore, their needs might be quite different from what adults expect. Giving them the opportunity and the venues to communicate their world is what a charrette can provide.

Social Issues and Experience. As America becomes increasingly culturally diverse, young people may experience life quite differently than we adults did. Kids today are more urbane; they deal with speed-of-light technology media and omnipresent popular culture. Their social experiences are most likely more varied. However, a charrette is still an opportunity to have young people from different backgrounds come together and share their perspectives. This very diversity among the participants and the range of their experiences can increase the credibility of what young people will explore in a charrette. Their suggested ideas and solutions have the potential for bringing a broader cross section of the community together than may be the case in a conventional planning process where participation may be more limited.

Solutions. Young people, who relate to life on the street, may have solutions that look different from City Hall's. Quite often, youth see themselves as part of the solution as a result of a charrette, which is healthier than being seen as part of the problem. In developing the charrette make certain you consider how the resulting plan or ideas incorporate young people in the solution.

A Fresh Look

Many times the motivation for a charrette is to have the community examine planning issues that have been overlooked. This is why the charrette can be a wonderful advocacy tool for adult planners. It can serve as a creative way to bring attention to a problem. Ideally, a youth charrette will provide perspective on current policies and highlight how they differ from the young person's view of what they should be. From this, a new direction could be established.

What Has Been Done. As a facilitator, one of your roles is to make sure the charrette is informed about current policies or plans. Teens in particular, can understand how to state their position relative to the current polices and practices. Discussing your charrette project in light of these policies and plans will help young people understand where they stand regarding their ideas. They should be able to ask themselves: "Are our ideas really different?"

How Policy Differs and Setting a New Direction. If the charrette sponsor or the youth participants want to use the results of the charrette to raise expectations of change, then they have to communicate how the recommendations differ from current policies. They need to be ready to explain to the community how this establishes a new direction. This is true for any type of planning problem, from a community comprehensive plan to revitalization of a street or neighborhood. In developing the final project and report, you and the participants need to ask: "How is our understanding of the issues and proposed solutions different from city hall?" and "What new directions does this charrette recommend?"

Informing the Adult Community

A youth charrette's fresh look at a local planning issue can create a new agenda for how community issues are approached. The results of the charrette should provide a story that can demonstrate to the adult community the importance of these issues and the benefits of a solution.

Raising Awareness. In many cases, a charrette may uncover an issue or public concern that has not concerned the policymakers. Awareness-raising is one of the most powerful effects of a charrette. Including in a presentation a few "did you know that's . . ." can be very hard hitting. These insights can be communicated with pictures, maps of existing conditions, summaries of youth-administered surveys, or clips, quotes, or segments from interviews that illustrate a point.

Communicate What Is Important. Make sure youth presenters emphasize what is important to them. It is hard for any adult policymaking body to ignore a passionate presentation about what is important for youth and families. This is especially true when the presentation is made by young people who clearly have their act together—the message is clear, the issues well articulated, the problems are well researched and analyzed, and the priorities are sharply focused.

COMMUNICATING YOUTH IDEAS AND PRIORITIES

Young people can make their views known in the press or other media, and can become powerful communicators and effective advocates.

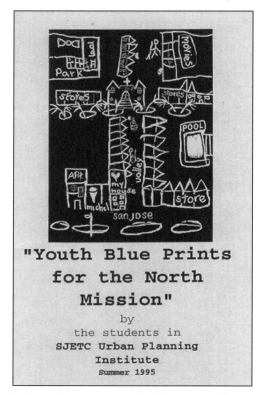

**"Youth Blue Prints
for the North
Mission"**

by
the students in
SJETC Urban Planning
Institute
Summer 1995

This project report served as the main tool for communicating with the sponsors and clients.

Youth as Communicators

In addition to creating their own media outreach plan and media materials, young people can develop their own events. They can be spokespersons at public hearings, visit the mayor and explain their position, make videos, and prepare printed materials for the media.

Post-Charrette Presentations. Charrettes are fun, but when it comes to making a presentation, it should be all business. The participants develop a script for an oral presentation and rehearse. In addition, the participants decide who will speak for them and how they want the presentation to be shaped. Generally, the presentation should include:

Purpose for the charrette
Overall process
Key issues
Potential solutions
Recommended actions

The presentation will have greater impact if it is well organized and provides concise recommended actions.

Teams. Have the kids present as a team. The team should be representative of the participants. The audience should have a sense of the types of young people that participated. Make sure each team member has a significant role and message.

The Message. As in any campaign, the presentation teams need to stay focused on the message. Make sure the team has their story straight. Make certain the key issues and recommendations are clearly summarized at the end of the presentation. Also, prepare the young people to answer questions. Establish the "team experts" to answer particular issues or select a spokesperson for the question segment.

Media Outreach Plan

In Chapter 4, we discussed a media plan as one exercise in the charrette. However, if the results of the charrette are to have a lasting impact, or support an ongoing advocacy effort, participants may want to take part in the implementation of a media and communications plan.

Types of Media Opportunities. There are a variety of media to be tapped by young people to get the word out. These include print and broadcast media of various scales.

Here are some to keep in mind:

- Newsletter: runs throughout the life of the project and is circulated to the sponsor and other groups affected by the planning project.
- News Releases: sent to local media regularly and contain eye-catching photographs.
- Article: prepared for the local newspaper with photographs.
- Web page: explains the project, reports its progress, and presents the final product.
- Exhibit or collage: displayed in some public area, such as a school hallway, local museum, community library, or vacant storefront.
- Community meeting: youth participants present their project and proposals to the general public.
- Video that records the main features of the charrette and its findings to show to fellow students, the sponsor, cable-access TV, and civic groups.

The Press Kit. With the help of a public relations specialist volunteer, young people can prepare a press kit. This includes a written summary/press release of the charrette; action photographs of the event; sample pictures, maps and graphics; and a list of contact people.

The Editorial Board. In some cases a visit to the local newspaper editorial board can be arranged. The purpose of the visit is to share the results of the charrette, as well as to learn how the media select and report on newsworthy stories. This offers a terrific learning experience for both sides. This can often be followed up by an op-ed piece from the youth that participated in the event.

ACTIVE YOUTH CITIZENS

For older children, charrettes can be used to prepare action plans.

Advocates for Youth

As part of a larger ongoing advocacy effort, charrettes can create a team of committed young people and sponsors. The charrette itself creates the agenda for their efforts.

Role of Kids' Helper. As facilitators and sponsors, adults play an important supporting role. Your "kids' helper" function goes beyond the charrette and into influencing the role young people will play in communities. You must become the *advocates* for the *advocates*. You will need to help create the media opportunities, venues, and audiences for their message.

Coalition for the Youth Agenda. In most communities there are a wide range of youth advocates and organizations. They can be found in school districts, churches, after-school programs, boys and girls clubs, and many other organizations. Charrettes offer a chance to bring these organizations together as sponsors. They can provide the venues for presenting the charrette results, and serve as champions for a youth agenda. Together, working on behalf young citizens, they can fashion a larger agenda for children, teens, and families in their communities. In this capacity, charrettes can become catalysts for partnerships and coalitions that support youth and their agenda.

Advocates for Funding

Many of the issues and ideas of charrette participants will require financial resources to carry out. This means public funding, private resources, or a combination must be brought to the task. In many cases, sweat equity and volunteer efforts can be recruited to carry out the ideas.

Public Money Is Public Policy. Remember, public resources reflect public policy and support. Many institutions and public agencies are strapped for resources and cannot easily fund youth initiative projects and programs. In some cases, agencies may consider a reallocation of resources to carry out a program. Other times, citizens, convinced of the worthiness of young peoples' ideas, may need to mount an aggressive campaign to not only gain acceptance for the ideas, but also to identify and develop revenue sources. This may include a sales tax or some other new source of funding. The best advocacy happens at a communitywide and policymaker level. A good question to ask young citizens and your cosponsors: "How would you plan a charrette and the post-charrette activities to attract financial support for the youth agenda?"

Private Sector Partnerships. There are many foundations and corporations with wonderful programs that finance youth issues. These private sector institutions can make excellent partners for co-sponsoring charrettes and implementing youth projects and programs. This will require an understanding of grant opportunities with foundations and finding the right match of project to funder. The communications plan, developed by the young people, can include a strategy for gaining financial support from the private sector. Charrette issues may be brought to the attention of funders through articles in the company's or organization's newsletter or a presentation to a company's public relations department or chief executive.

Volunteers. In many communities, youth and adult volunteers make a huge difference. They clean parks; form neighborhood watch teams; mentor, coach, teach, and advise; and provide a myriad of other activities that improve the lives of young people. A question for you and your team as you design your charrette: "How can the talents of volunteers in the community be motivated and harnessed for your program?"

Ongoing Advocacy

As we have said before, a charrette can be a one-time event or part of a larger process. In the case of the latter, a charrette can provide a benchmark. The results of the charrette can serve as in-progress or preliminary recommendations for an ongoing youth planning effort. Over time, a new generation of charrettes can be used to address new issues and move the project or issues along. The agenda for each charrette would reflect the new set of objectives. This might include:

◆ support for the project or program.
◆ new co-sponsors and alliances.
◆ new venues for learning and public awareness.
◆ allowing the next generation of youth to define their agenda.

In the larger context, educational, youth advocacy, and community planning charrettes are a powerful tool. With careful planning, young citizens can hone their communication skills, get a hands-on civic studies course, and empower themselves to make a difference.

CHAPTER 6

LESSONS LEARNED

CONVEY A REALISTIC VIEW OF THE PUBLIC DECISION-MAKING PROCESS

Roger Hart in his book, *Children's Participation,* makes an excellent point about not overselling the efficacy of planning. He believes that if we are sincere in teaching young people about real citizenship then we have to be honest about how difficult it is to bring about certain kinds of change or address major problems. Elected leaders may listen politely and not be the least bit persuaded to take action in line with the young peoples' suggestions. But that is the reality of the planning process. Not all decisions are based on planning. A well-defined and articulate plan may not provide the road map to community change. In short, we should not oversell the power of planning.

That does not mean we should throw up our hands and say, "I told you so." Rather, we should build into the charrette some realistic discussion about how plans come about. Also, it is likely that a charrette that addresses a manageable problem will give young people a better chance of bringing about change.

Hart is equally skeptical of young peoples' participation that is done largely for public relations purposes. We certainly need to create an awareness of cities and city planning issues but, Hart says, some efforts to involve kids in planning are merely eyewash. The planners undertake the project to get good press coverage or to create something appealing to the general public. Too often, the results are not taken seriously and the event was a media stunt. Of course, there is nothing wrong about advertising projects to the media, or for having some fun yourself while working on the project. But, it is critical that you be honest with yourself about what you are trying to achieve.

And, even good projects may have some limited effects---—like many things in life, not all ideas will take root and flourish.

Here are some lessons we can share with you about things that might go wrong.

MAKE CERTAIN YOUR PARTNERS ARE COMMITTED

Remember the lesson on keeping up the energy level in the charrette? Well, energy is needed for the pre-charrette planning stages as well. You need to be a strong leader and use your enthusiasm as the catalyst for the project.

It may be helpful to test the level of commitment of your partners by giving them assignments in the planning stages. You may be able to detect that you have a problem if the assignment does not get done. At that point you need to decide whether or not you will shoulder more responsibility. For example, a teacher may be enthusiastic in the first meeting, but not follow through with the warm-up exercise. As the charrette leader, you may need to step in and ask for time to visit with the students in the classroom and conduct the exercise in advance of the charrette. Or, you need to spend more time coaching the teacher, setting deadlines, and checking up on the work. In short, you will need to manage the project.

Or you may be the teacher and have some reservations about your planners. Again, test them with an assignment and be prepared to recruit more planners or shift responsibilities.

ENSURE EVERYONE UNDERSTANDS THE GOALS

It is all too easy to assume everyone understands your project only to find out at some critical moment when things are falling apart, that is hardly the case. Prepare a short statement of purpose and goals to hand out to the principal players, such as the school principal or curriculum coordinator. In your discussions with these people, repeat the goals and everyone's role from time to time.

In cases where you are uncertain about the perspective of your principal players, try drafting a *letter of agreement* that outlines what you are trying to accomplish and each principal player's obligation to the project. Again, discuss this and make certain everyone has agreed to it.

Be as articulate as possible about education goals so everyone knows what to expect from the live charrette event.

CONTINUE COMMUNICATION THROUGHOUT THE ENTIRE PROJECT

Regular communication with the key players or stakeholders is critical. And much of that communication needs to be direct, on the phone, through e-mail, or face to face. Don't ever assume that simply sending a letter gets the job done. You need to follow up and keep the communication going throughout the process.

Since it is likely that you will be working with adults who are volunteering their time, make certain you are organized and prepared. Don't waste valuable time by not being prepared. Break all tasks down into manageable stages, and don't overwhelm any volunteer with too much work or responsibility.

Don't be afraid to ask for more help when you need it, and don't forget to plan for enough volunteers so you or the organizer are not overwhelmed.

LEAVE ROOM FOR FLEXIBILITY

There are times that even the best organized event will go astray. Leave time in your schedule for unexpected mishaps or longer than anticipated discussions. Improvise when need be. Of course, it is easy to advise this in a book, and much more challenging to do it live. However, good preparation should allow you the ability to relax during the charrette and respond to unexpected happenstance. Besides, you never know, someone may come up with a better idea! And you don't want to waste good ideas.

PREP YOUR CHARRETTE TEAM WELL

Hold briefing meetings and build some camaraderie among all the adult participants. Reward them with a little food, praise, and an enjoyable event. Make certain all the adults have written instructions and copies of the charrette workbook. They should have enough support material that they can turn to it quickly when need be—and when you are not available to answer questions.

Also, the adults may want some sort of post-charrette celebration to help them unwind, share insights, and savor the fun. Food and drink is every bit as good a reward for adults as it is for young people. Don't forget, they will want to share with you something about their experience, so by all means, give them an opportunity to do just that.

In the last chapter, we have provided you with an exercise to design your own charrette. Let us share one final piece of advice—enjoy!

CHAPTER 7

DESIGNING YOUR OWN KIDS' CHARRETTE

This is an exercise for you to complete. Now that you've finished reading the guide, it's time to design your own charrette.

ASSIGNMENT

◆ Identify your potential planning topics
◆ Identify the age group of the young participants
◆ Identify your education and planning goals
◆ Identify your client, host, and volunteers
◆ Identify your research scheme
◆ Develop two exercises for the charrette

STEP ONE

Begin by identifying your potential topics for your charrette, based on the current situation in your home community, or the community in which you will be conducting the charrette.

a) _____

_____

b) _____

_____

c) _____

_____

d) _____

_____

STEP TWO

Consult a colleague or one of your potential partners and discuss which of these topics would work best for a charrette. Select one.

_____

STEP THREE

List the age group with which you will work.

_____

STEP FOUR

List three education and planning goals for this charrette.

a) _____

b) _____

c) _____

STEP FIVE

Identify your client(s).

_____

_____

_____

_____

Identify your host institution and the people you will need to work with.

a) _____

_____

b) _____

_____

List your potential volunteers and Kids' Assistants

_____

_____

STEP SIX

Identify your research scheme. List the kinds of information your participants will collect and how.

a) _____

_____

b) _____

_____

c) _____

_____

d) _____

_____

STEP SEVEN

Design two exercises for this charrette.

Exercise One

Exercise Two

Publications Cited in the Text

Beasant, Pam, and Alastair Smith. *How to Draw Maps and Charts*. Tulsa, Okla.: Usborne (EDC Publishing), n.d. Price: $4.95.

Gralla, Preston. *How Cities Work*. Emeryville, Cal.: Siff-Davis Press, 1995. Price $19.95.

Hart, Roger A. *Children's Participation: The Theory and Practice of Involving Young Citizens in Community Development and Environmental Care*. London: Earthscan Publications, Ltd. and New York: UNICEF, 1997. Price: £18.95. Also available from Children's Environmental Research Group, City University of New York, 212-642-2970.

Lewis, Barbara. *The Kid's Guide to Service Projects*. Minneapolis: Free Spirit Press, 1995. Price $10.95. Available through APA Planners Book Service, 312-431-9100.

————. *The Kid's Guide to Social Action*. Minneapolis: Free Spirit Press, 1991. Price $14.95.

Parker, Philip. *Global Cities: Investigating the Ecology of Our Towns and Cities*. New York: Thomson Learning, 1995. Price $15.95

Taylor, Barbara. *Maps and Mapping*. New York: Kingfisher Books, 1992. Price $6.95.

von Tscharner, Renata, and Ronald Lee Fleming. *A Changing American Cityscape*. Dale Seymour Publications, 1993. Price $36.95.

Products Available from APA's Planners Book Service (Prices and availability subject to change.)
To order:
Planners Book Service
122 S. Michigan Ave., Ste. 1600
Chicago, IL 60603
phone: 312-431-9100
fax 312-431-9985
www.planning.org

Dilemmas of Development. Urban Land Institute, 1990. Price $55
A complete role simulation package (scenario, site map, teacher's guide, student handouts, video, evaluation) on planning and development process designed for high school juniors and seniors; the roles are well-written and can be simplified for a younger audience.

Brown, Nancy Benziger, ed. *Planning Education Kids Style*. APA Tennessee Chapter, 1994. Price $35
A manual with step-by-step instructions to introduce planning and design concepts in the classroom, including hands-on activities where students build a city; includes an accompanying how-to video; for grades 3-6.

UrbanPlan. Urban Land Institute, 1991. Price $60
A high school curriculum package on redevelopment of an urban neighborhood includes video of actual redevelopment project; students break into competing development teams to respond to a mock request for proposals.

Mullahey, Ramona K. *Community as a Learning Resource*. 1994. Price $69
A variety of lesson ideas and hands-on exercises to guide teachers and planners; uses the immediate community as a classroom to learn about planning, architecture, design, preservation, archaeology, community issues; activities are sequenced by grade level or can be used as stand alone for grades K-12; includes other suggested resources and a 30-minute how-to video presenting two educational modules based on *Dilemmas of Development* and *Box City*.

Walk Around the Block. Center for Understanding the Built Environment, 1992. Price $35
A ready-to-use curriculum to help teach children about city planning, architecture,

history, mapping; kids learn to "read" their neighborhood in a variety of ways and advocate for making a difference in their community; written for grades 3-7, and adaptable for all ages.

Other Products and Publications

Little Planner™ 1982, Leisure Learning Products, Inc. Price $19.95
Board game for ages 3-6

Mandel, Linda, and Hedi M. Mandel. *The Treasure of Trash*. Avery Publishing Group, 1993. Price $15.00
Book geared to grades K-3

Other Organizations with Published Materials

Center for Understanding the Built Environment (C.U.B.E.)
5328 W. 67th St.
Prairie Village, KS 66208
913-262-0691

Box City curriculum
Walk Around the Block curriculum (see above)
Hometown U.S.A., computer program
The Kid's Guide to Social Action, book with exercises and projects
Architecture and Children, curriculum posters and teachers guide
Historic Preservation Education, curriculum
Architecture in Education, book
ArchiTeacher, curriculum

National Endowment for the Arts
Arts in Education Program
1100 Pennsylvania Ave., NW
Washington, DC 20506
202-682-5426

What Is Design? poster

ILLUSTRATION CREDITS

Cover
Artville; Kids' Art

Foreword
Bruce Race (v, vii); Neighborhood News-*Garfield Heights Tribune* (viii); Maps and Geography Division, Library of Congress (x); Sarout Long (xi); Alex Barios (xiii)

Chapter 1
Clay Campbell (1, 22); Candace Kane (3, 4); Cooper Hewitt/National Design Museum (6, 7); Bruce Race (8, 9, 10, 11, 12, 13, 15, 18, 19, 20, 21, 26, 29); Carolyn Torma (16); American Planning Association (24)

Chapter 2
Carolyn Torma (31, 35); American Planning Association (32); Bruce Race (34, 36, 38); Candace Kane (40)

Chapter 3
Noré Winter (45, 48, 58); Linda Bernhardt (46); Carolyn Torma (49, 56, 59); Candace Kane (50); Bruce Race (53, 55, 57)

Chapter 4
Bruce Race (69, 70, 71, 73, 76); Clay Campbell (74); *San Diego Union-Tribune* (75)

Chapter 5
Clay Campbell (77); Bruce Race (80)